ISSUES IN POLITICAL THEORY

Political Theory has undergone a remarkable development in recent years. From a state in which it was once declared dead, it has come to occupy a central place in the study of Politics. Both political ideas and the wide-ranging arguments to which they give rise are now treated in a rigorous, analytical fashion, and political theorists have contributed to disciplines as diverse as economics, sociology and law. These developments have made the subject more challenging and exciting, but they have also added to the difficulties of students and others coming to the subject for the first time. Much of the burgeoning literature in specialist books and journals is readily intelligible only to those who are already well-versed in the subject.

Issues in Political Theory is a series conceived in response to this situation. It consists of a number of detailed and comprehensive studies of issues central to Political Theory which take account of the latest developments in scholarly debate. While making original contributions to the subject, books in the series are written especially for those who are new to Political Theory. Each volume aims to introduce its readers to the intricacies of a fundamental political issue and to help them find their way through the detailed, and often complicated, argument that that issue has attracted.

PETER JONES
ALBERT WEALE

ISSUES IN POLITICAL THEORY

Series Editors: PETER JONES and ALBERT WEALE

Published

David Beetham: **Legitimacy**
Christopher J. Berry: **Human Nature**
Tom Campbell: **Justice**
Tim Gray: **Freedom**
John Horton: **Political Obligation**
Michael Lessnoff: **Social Contract**
Richard Lindley: **Autonomy**
Susan Mendus: **Toleration and the Limits of Liberalism**
Andrew Reeve: **Property**

Forthcoming

Peter Jones: **Rights**
Raymond Plant: **Equality**
Hillel Steiner: **Utilitarianism**
Albert Weale: **Democracy**

Series Standing Order

If you would like to receive future titles in this series as they are published,
you can make use of our standing order facility. To place a standing order
please contact your bookseller or, in case of difficulty, write to us at the
address below with your name and address and the name of the series.
Please state with which title you wish to begin your standing order.
(If you live outside the UK we may not have the rights for your area,
in which case we will forward your order to the publisher concerned.)

Customer Services Department, Macmillan Distribution Ltd,
Houndmills, Basingstoke, Hampshire, RG21 2XS, England

Political Obligation

John Horton

MACMILLAN

First published 1992 by
THE MACMILLAN PRESS LTD
Houndmills, Basingstoke, Hampshire RG21 2XS
and London
Companies and representatives
throughout the world

ISBN 0–333–36784–7 hardcover
ISBN 0–333–36785–5 paperback

A catalogue record for this book is available
from the British Library

Copy-edited and typeset by Povey–Edmondson
Okehampton and Rochdale, England

Printed in Hong Kong

For Christopher

Contents

Preface and Acknowledgements

The aim of this book is to introduce a range of philosophical questions and arguments concerning political obligation. It does not aspire to be a comprehensive treatment of its subject, nor does it offer a precisely articulated and fully developed argument of its own. My principal focus is on the various attempts by political philosophers to provide a justification of political obligation, and in consequence other issues have been more or less neglected. However, while not the only interesting aspect of political obligation, the question of justification has been fundamental within most philosophical discussions of the topic and lies at the heart of any systematic treatment of it. Most of the book is taken up with the attempt to sketch the more prominent arguments about the justification of political obligation; to explore some of their assumptions and implications; and to suggest what seem to me to be their most significant weaknesses and limitations. The approach adopted is analytical rather than historical, and my concern to address arguments of particular relevance in the modern world is reflected to some extent both in the choice of, and in the relative space devoted to, the positions discussed.

Much of the book, therefore, is concerned with the critical exposition of the ideas of others, and in undertaking this task I have sought to achieve a reasonable balance between exposition and criticism, and between fidelity and accessibility. It is inevitable that some parts of the book are more difficult than others; but I am especially conscious, in consequence of my desire to avoid excessive exposition of canonical texts in political philosophy and to relate them to a contemporary perspective, that the richness and complexity of many of these accounts of political obligation receive less than justice. Such failings are relatively easily remedied by reading the originals, and by reference to some of the many secondary commentaries which are now available on all the principal figures in the history of Western political philosophy. However, while much of the book takes the form of a critical survey, it would be misleading to imply that it is not informed by an authorial point of view.

This point of view encompasses both a conception of political philosophy and a specific approach to the problem of political obligation. So far as political philosophy is concerned, I am deeply sceptical of the more ambitious claims which have been made on its behalf by some of its practitioners: I favour a view of political philosophy which sees it as seeking to help us understand ourselves and our place in the world rather than aiming, for example, to provide rational 'proofs' of particular political commitments. Such an approach certainly need not be uncritical, but in my view most of the interesting arguments in political philosophy are better or worse, more or less plausible, and only rarely true or false. With respect to political obligation I have tried to offer an interpretation which avoids at least some of the unsatisfactory features of other accounts, in particular those that I call voluntarist theories, yet does not succumb to the scepticism about political obligation which has become increasingly prevalent in the philosophical literature. I hope, therefore, that these features may give the book a somewhat wider interest than simply the student audience to whom it is primarily addressed. In particular, I hope it may encourage others to explore these ideas further.

For a work of fairly modest aspirations this book has been an unreasonably long time in both gestation and writing, and in the process I have acquired a great many debts of gratitude. Inevitably a book of this sort draws extensively on the work of previous writers: I have done my best to acknowledge such debts in the references, but I should apologise for those which I have inadvertently overlooked. My interest in the problem of political obligation goes back nearly twenty years to when I was a student, and it is a loss to the reader, in addition to being a source of personal regret, that this book was unable to benefit from the astute and wise criticism of the late John Rees, one of my earliest and most inspiring teachers. However, I have been very fortunate to have had the help and support of so many other people. The University of York has provided a mostly congenial environment for my work, despite the best efforts of the British government during the last decade to sabotage the effective functioning of the university system. It has been particularly fruitful to have been part of the Morrell Studies in Toleration in the Department of Politics, which through the generous support of the

C. & J. B. Morrell Trust has sponsored a stimulating programme of research in political philosophy. This support has also helped to attract many outstanding graduate students, whom it has been a pleasure to teach and from whom I have learnt a good deal. I should like to thank the Trustees for their continued support, and in particular Nicholas Morrell, Edward Goodman and Geoffrey Heselton.

The book had its origins principally in work now contained in Chapter 6, which in earlier forms was presented at Durham, Swansea and New College, Oxford, and I am grateful for the useful discussion it received on each occasion. Both that chapter and drafts of Chapters 2 and 5 were presented at Political Theory Workshops at the University of York, and subsequently appeared as *Morrell Discussion Papers*. These meetings, and I refer not only to those when my own work was the subject of attention, have been an invaluable source of intellectual stimulation, in which constructively critical discussion has been sustained in a serious yet relaxed and sympathetic context. I am grateful to all the participants over the years. Among the many people with whom I have discussed political obligation, or who have commented on parts of the book, I should like to thank especially Alex Callinicos, David Edwards, Margaret Gilbert, Terry Hopton, Preston King, John Liddington, Barbara McGuinness, David Morland and Rian Voet. No author could have had a more cheerfully long-suffering publisher than Steven Kennedy; Keith Povey has been a constructive copy-editor; and the two academic editors of the series in which this volume appears have been models of tactful support: Albert Weale was especially encouraging in the early stages, and Peter Jones read a complete draft of the text, making numerous characteristically acute and perceptive suggestions. I have also benefited enormously from the very helpful comments of Paul Kelly, Chris Megone, Glen Newey and Igor Primoratz, all of whom read the complete manuscript in draft and saved me from many confusions and errors. So too did Peter Nicholson and Susan Mendus, but my intellectual and personal debts to them go very much deeper. Peter Nicholson, initially my teacher and now a colleague and friend, has encouraged me and commented on my work all my academic life, a labour on his part for which I am sincerely grateful. Susan Mendus and I have collaborated on several projects during the last decade, and her tireless encouragement, sympathy and support – friendship in the fullest sense – in addition to her perceptive criticism, has been indispensable to me. Of course none of these people is to blame for the use to which I have put their help, and all deserved better.

Much of this book was written during what were difficult times for me personally. In addition to Chris Megone, Peter Nicholson and Susan Mendus I should also like to thank in this context: John Crump, Pamela Dowswell, Adrian Leftwich, Jackie Morgan, Dorothy Nott and particularly Keith Alderman. Alison, Anna, Karen, Mike, Nick, Tina, Steve Reilly and especially Claire Roberts also helped, as too did Lynne and Christopher. However, above all my personal thanks are owed to Jenny Bradford. I am also grateful to her for typing some of the manuscript in its early stages; and to Jackie Morgan who undertook the bulk of this work, and whose patience with my incessant revisions was infinite.

University of York   *John Horton*

1 Introduction

The term 'political obligation' is not one with much currency in contemporary life outside of books and discussions of political philosophy; and even in that context it appears to date from as recently as the late nineteenth century (Green, 1986). It would be a mistake, however, to conclude from this that the complex of issues which the term denotes are of recent origin, or that it is the concern only of professional philosophers and is merely 'academic' in the pejorative sense. The cluster of questions and issues with which it is concerned lies at the heart of political life and has done so, with greater or lesser urgency and self-consciousness, for as long as people have reflected upon their relationship to the political community of which they are members. It is this relationship, as I shall go on to explain, which is fundamental to an understanding of the problem of political obligation. In this chapter my purpose is to introduce the problem, to sketch some important preliminary distinctions, and to indicate in general terms the concerns of this book. I shall begin, however, by trying to show in a very simple way both the kind of issues involved in political obligation and why they matter. The task of characterising a more refined and precise understanding of political obligation will be left until the final section of the chapter.

Political obligation as a problem

Probably everyone reading these words is a member of a particular political entity (today almost certainly a state) and all our lives are crucially shaped and structured in a multiplicity of ways by this apparently simple fact. Even the most resolutely unpolitical people will have to recognise that the nature of the political community in which they live, what it demands of them and what it permits them, is crucial to their living the lives they do. Where citizens are generally content with the political arrangements of their society or are satisfied with their own position within it, they may not

1

choose and will not be compelled to reflect upon their relationship to the political community of which they are members. Many features of this relationship may be taken for granted, and meeting the requirements which it imposes upon us may often become unreflective and habitual: we pay our taxes, apply for a passport if we wish to travel abroad, complete our census returns and much else. In this respect our relationship to our political community is like many other relationships and commitments – familial, professional, religious and so on – in being experienced as an important but often practically unproblematic feature of our daily lives. However, we are all equally aware that these relationships and commitments can become deeply problematic and troubling. They can give rise to questions which require us to rethink our sense of who we are and what we should do, and in this way they can radically transform our lives.

It is only to be expected, therefore, that people will become most conscious of their relationship to their political community when, for whatever reason, it becomes problematic: that people's lives are intimately bound up with the wider polity will probably become a cause for reflection, for example, should demands be made of them or prohibitions imposed upon them that they find unacceptable. It is for this reason, primarily, that it is in times of political crisis, of serious dissent or discontent, of social breakdown or dislocation, that political obligation is most likely to become a central feature of political debate and activity. It is in circumstances such as these that people are most likely to question the authority of their government and to think seriously about the terms and basis of their relationship to their political community. In particular we may come to ask what legitimate claims the political community has on us; what we owe it; and how both these matters are to be determined. It is in this way that we are most likely to be led to reflecting *generally* on our relationship to our political community, and that the need for some philosophical account of political obligation is likely to be felt most acutely. Yet, though it is in circumstances such as these that political obligation will most probably be experienced as a *problem*, it is to less troubled times that we must look for an 'answer'. It is a familiar irony that it is in circumstances in which our need for an answer to our questions is most pressing, that it is most difficult to give one. This is undoubtedly one of the impulses to philosophy.

It is, therefore, not surprising to find that political philosophers' sense of the importance of the problem of political obligation has varied with changing circumstances and that philosophising about it has often been most intense when some people have found themselves to be in radical conflict with their political community or when the political community itself has been perceived to be close to dissolution. Thus, for example, one of the earliest sustained philosophical discussions of what we would recognise as the prôblem of political obligation occurs in the context of Plato's report of Socrates' meditations on his relationship to the Athenian *polis* which had condemned him to death in the fourth century BC. Encouraged by his friends to escape and seek exile outside his *polis*, rejecting the possibility of giving up his vocation in life to appease his critics, Socrates reflects on what his obligations to Athens require of him. He considers a range of arguments, many of which continue to reverberate to the present time, and concludes that 'you must do whatever your city and country command, or else persuade it in accordance with universal justice' and that unlawful resistance would be wrong (Plato, 1969, p. 91). In Socrates' case his own arguments therefore required him to accept his execution. Thus, whatever the merits of his particular arguments, Socrates shows us the seriousness of the issues: ultimately political obligation may be a matter of life or death.

Another era in which the problem of political obligation seemed especially acute was seventeenth-century England. In a country riven by religious conflict and civil war, involving armed insurrection and the execution of the King, the work of Thomas Hobbes and John Locke emerged as an attempt to formulate an account of political obligation which would help to hold together a country apparently on the verge of chaos and disintegration. In this context, one of the most formidable and enduring traditions of thought about political obligation, the social contract tradition, developed as a way of thinking about the relations between the individual and the polity. While the idea of a contract between the polity and its citizens is clearly present among Socrates' arguments in the *Crito*, it is in response to the breakdown of an essentially religiously sanctioned political order and the emergence of new forms of individualism in the seventeenth century (not only in England) that this approach begins to be more fully explored. Furthermore, in so far as the potential for antagonism between individual autonomy and judgement, on the one hand, and the demands made by the state on the other, has not merely persisted but been sharpened by subsequent historical developments, then the problem of political obligation may become more rather than less pressing. It is not, therefore, a problem which is of concern only to earlier generations. We need only consider the recent tumultuous events in Eastern Europe, a variety of modern nationalisms and recurrent civil wars to survey a panorama of contemporary contexts within which political obligation is experienced as deeply problematic. Furthermore, while situations of radical conflict or political dislocation provide the most dramatic instances, there are less extreme but none the less serious examples of circumstances where political obligation becomes uncomfortably troubling. A good case would be that of many loyal young United States citizens in the 1960s and early 1970s drafted into the army to fight on behalf of their country in what they believed to be a deeply unjust war in Vietnam.

All these events and situations are inevitably extraordinarily complex and it would be fatuous to attempt to incorporate all these complexities within one simple notion of political obligation. At their heart, however, lies a cluster of questions which are also central to an understanding of political obligation: What political community does one belong to? How is membership of a polity determined? What duties or obligations does one have by virtue of one's membership? How are those duties or obligations to be judged relative to other commitments and obligations? The answers to these, and other similar, questions are central to any understanding of political obligation. Moreover, political philosophers have tended to see one question as fundamental: on what basis, in terms of what reasons, should we legitimately ascribe political obligations to people? It is this question of justification or explanation – and it is not always possible to separate them – which is the focus of most philosophical discussions of political obligation and of this book.

One problem or many?

The idea that there is one problem of political obligation which different political philosophers at different times have sought to answer is, however, open to serious objection. This objection is encapsulated in the claim that there is nothing which can be identified as *the* problem of political obligation but only a succession of historically different and distinct problems. It is argued that it is grossly anachronistic, and hence misleading, to think that Socrates' problem in Athens, Hobbes' or Locke's problems in seventeenth-century England, or the problem of a political philosopher today are all the *same* problem, or that it is useful to describe them all as concerned with political obligation. There is certainly some truth in this view: we cannot simply pretend that Socrates, Hobbes and the political philosopher today are all contemporaries joined in a single debate. Their social and political circumstances, background beliefs and assumptions, and even their conception of argument will vary, and these differences cannot simply be ignored. However, it would be mistaken to conclude on the basis of these genuine and important differences that we cannot, to some extent at least, not merely come to understand the concerns which exercised Socrates but also relate them to our own circumstances and problems.

This is not a straightforward matter and it requires both historical sensitivity and philosophical acuity. It would be absurd, for example, to treat a young American in the 1960s facing the draft to fight in Vietnam as being in the identical situation to Socrates in Athens in the fourth century BC. Yet, at a certain level of generality (and some level of generality is unavoidable), it is not obviously absurd to see some similarities in their predicaments; to see how what Socrates says about his situation might relate to that of the potential conscript. This is possible because, while they are separated by historical circumstances, they share a human condition in which reconciling the claims of the individual with those of the larger political community to which they belong is a problem which has the potential to arise wherever people are members of political communities, and are also capable of distinguishing themselves from it. So while there are many significant differences, for example, between the way in which the problem of political obligation is formulated and interpreted in ancient and modern political philosophy, we can still trace a kinship of concerns (O'Sullivan, 1987, Ch. 1). The arguments of earlier philosophers are variously developed and rejected by later philosophers, and most philosophers, whether or not mistakenly, have believed themselves to be presenting accounts of political obligation of very much wider relevance than their own specific historical circumstances.

There is, therefore, no reason to think that we are forced to choose between these two extreme positions. It is not the case either that there is one perennial, unchanging, identical problem which constitutes *the* problem of political obligation, or that because every historical situation is in some sense unique there can be *no* common concerns which transcend such variable circumstances. There can be identity in difference; the precise form in which questions pertaining to political obligation present themselves will inevitably vary, as will the answers, yet they can also be recognised as related to similar or overlapping concerns. Such considerations also apply to social and cultural differences existing at the same historical time: the questions confronting a Republican in Northern Ireland, a draftee in the US, and a black South African are all very different, but this does not preclude a significant continuity of concerns. Philosophers certainly need to be alert and sensitive to historical and cultural differences but they need also to identify the general in the particular and to seek out similarities and connections. The question of precisely how much it is possible to say about political obligation in general, and to what extent understanding needs to be contextualised and related concretely to specific historical circumstances is itself an issue which must be investigated. There is, however, no reason to begin such an enquiry by assuming that it is impossible to say *anything* about political obligation in general.

Political obligation, therefore, is fundamentally concerned with the relationship between people and the political community of which they are members. It gives rise to questions of considerable practical and philosophical importance concerning the obligations or duties one has in virtue of one's membership of a particular polity. How does this affect one's relations with other members and how do they differ from those of non-members? What is one's relationship to the political authority, to law and to the institutions and personnel of government? These are all questions which can be raised at a more or less general, or more or less specific, level. The kind of answers which they can be given is itself a subject of philosophical dispute. In fact I shall conclude that there are considerable limits to what can be said about political obligation in general, but this should be understood as the outcome of the argument rather than as a presupposition of it. In part, however, what is at issue in such a debate about the scope of philosophical arguments is the nature of philosophy or, as it principally concerns us, political philosophy itself. It is to a preliminary consideration of this issue that we must now turn; leaving until the final section further clarification and refinement of the problem of political obligation.

Political philosophy

This book is a work of political philosophy not political sociology or history. Though it contains both historical and sociological considerations, it does not aim to offer either an historical narrative of changing relations between individuals and their particular polity or a sociological explanation of the way such relations actually operate. It is not concerned with explaining why in fact people obey the law, interesting and worthwhile though such an enquiry is in its own right (Tyler, 1990). Nor does this book attempt a complete or systematic history of ideas about political obligation, although the ideas of some of the principal figures in the history of political philosophy figure prominently in the ensuing discussion. Disciplinary boundaries, such as those between history, sociology and philosophy, are sometimes regarded as obstacles to a proper or clear understanding of issues , because they lead to a fragmentation of knowledge. However, while it cannot be denied that an over-insistence on narrow disciplinary perspectives can have this effect, different disciplines characteristically address different sorts of question. This is not to suggest that history or sociology are always irrelevant to political philosophy: for example, historical misunderstanding or insensitivity can sometimes make for poor political philosophy. The point which needs to be appreciated is that each discipline should be assessed on its own terms and in relation to its own goals or purposes. It is pointless to judge philosophy as if it were history, and vice-versa.

In describing this as a work of political philosophy I intend to indicate that it attempts to explore the problem of political obligation through the interpretation of concepts and an assessment of the persuasiveness of various moral arguments and not through empirical investigations. It aims to give an account of the meaning of political obligation; to assess the merits of various arguments for and against it; and generally to contribute to an understanding of its moral significance and place in political life. However, beyond this level of rather anodyne generality about political philosophy, the nature of the activity is itself somewhat controversial and disputed. In this book I shall to some extent take sides on some of these disputes, defending one conception of political philosophy and expressing doubts about some of the more ambitious claims of some of its practitioners. However, this is a subsidiary concern, and much of the subsequent discussion will involve an unavoidable compromise between assessing various philosophical accounts of political obligation on their own terms, and questioning those terms. The approach adopted, therefore, inclines towards the inclusive rather than the exclusive. In any case it is perhaps a mistake, though a tempting one, to think that philosophical enquiry must conform to one narrow and circumscribed view of it. For philosophers, including political philosophers, have often understood and pursued their enquiries in different ways, many of which might with equal plausibility be regarded as genuinely philosophical.

Philosophy is a broad church, though it is true that, historically, the scope of philosophy generally has tended to narrow in the sense that, for example, some of what were once thought of as philosophical issues are now believed properly to belong to the province of the natural sciences. In the area of political philosophy it has also sometimes been claimed that much, if not all, of its traditional area of concern similarly belongs to the social sciences. (Such claims were, for example, an important motivating force in the development of 'political science'.) There is, it should be recognised, some truth in these claims, but not as much as the social sciences' more enthusiastic proponents have asserted. In so far as many political philosophers have engaged in ill-informed or out-dated sociological and historical speculation, then these tasks are appropriately seen as more properly belonging to the disciplines of sociology and history. However, two points are worth observing. First, these activities far from exhaust the traditional concerns of political philosophy. Secondly, it is arguable that the social sciences necessarily include a substantial philosophical dimension. I shall say a little more about each of these points, beginning with the second.

Much social scientific enquiry, despite pretensions to being closely modelled on the natural sciences, involves complex conceptual issues concerned with the meaning and interpretation of human actions, institutions and beliefs. These cannot be treated as unproblematic empirical data. The point here is not merely that all observation presupposes some conceptual structure or, as it is sometimes put, that all observation is theory-dependent, for that is as true of the natural sciences as it is of the social sciences. Rather, it is that human actions and beliefs are in part irreducibly bound up with their meaning and cannot be identified simply in terms of physical movements or spatio-temporal coordinates. For example, voting can be embodied in different physical movements (e.g. raising a hand, nodding the head, putting a cross on a piece of paper, etc.) and these same physical movements can have diverse meanings (e.g. respectively a desire to ask a question, a friendly greeting or a game of noughts and crosses, etc.). Voting, therefore, cannot be identified simply by reference to a particular type of physical movement. The meaning of an action cannot be understood without also understanding the complex structure of the other beliefs and activities which situate the action in its practical and conceptual context. The process of conceptual elucidation, which forms at least a necessary prelude to further empirical enquiry, and which is often inextricably bound up with it, has close affinities with the kind of enquiry which, as is argued below, is central to philosophy. Thus, just as, for instance, poor history can sometimes make for poor political philosophy, so sometimes philosophical naïveté can make for misguided social science.

The more important point, however, in the context of this book is that there remains a legitimate area of political philosophy which is not superseded by the social sciences. This is, in its largest sense, the area of conceptual and logical enquiry: exploring the meaning of political practices and beliefs; their consistency and coherence; their implications and relations to other beliefs; and their presuppositions and underlying assumptions. Thus my understanding of conceptual enquiry is significantly less narrow than what has become known as 'linguistic analysis' (Weldon, 1953; Miller, 1983). However, even allowing for this broader interpretation many political philosophers, both today and in the past, while not denying that these were legitimate philosophical tasks, would argue that this conception of political philosophy is unduly limited and restrictive. In particular, they would claim that political philosophy is concerned to develop normative moral and political theories; that is, theories which aspire not merely to understand and logically evaluate particular concepts and beliefs but also directly to guide political practice. Though myself deeply sceptical of some of these more ambitious claims for political philosophy, the issues are undeniably complex and probably impossible to settle to everyone's satisfaction. They will not be taken further in this Introduction, though differences about the nature of political philosophy will unavoidably surface in the course of subsequent discussion and they will need to be engaged with as and when they arise. Indeed, it is perhaps not too much of an exaggeration to claim that the ensuing discussion of political obligation is also more obliquely and incompletely a consideration of the possibilities and limits of political philosophy. I shall briefly return to some of the issues which this raises in the Conclusion, but before leaving this topic I shall first indicate very briefly what is involved in political philosophy conceived as conceptual enquiry by trying to rebut three possible objections (see Horton, 1984).

First, logical and conceptual enquiry need not be uncritical. In trying to make sense of our concepts and beliefs, there is no guarantee that we shall be successful. Concepts may be shown to be ambiguous or confused, and in exploring the consistency and coherence of beliefs it may be that contradictions, inconsistencies and incoherences are revealed. Where this is the case, there may be a variety of legitimate responses available, but among these is a radical reassessment of those beliefs which may involve the repudiation of some or the reconstruction of others. At the very least where philosophers claim to detect significant conceptual confusions or contradictory beliefs, this constitutes a challenge to provide a more coherent account of them. Hence conceptual and logical investigations need not serve to justify our ordinary modes of understanding and acting. There is, therefore, nothing necessarily uncritical or conservative about this kind of enquiry.

Second, and connectedly, though logical and conceptual enquiry ought properly to be an unbiased and disinterested investigation, this does not mean that it cannot have moral and political implications. These may result from beliefs being shown to be inconsistent or incoherent, or from following through to their conclusion the implications of beliefs which had not been fully appreciated or understood. If, for example, some combination of political beliefs can be shown to be contradictory, then this must have important practical implications for those who subscribe to those beliefs. Moreover, when we are dealing with tensions, ambiguities or ambivalences, or with more or less unacceptable implications of beliefs, rather than contradictions, as is more common in political philosophy, people may still rightly be disturbed by such revelations. They may, for example, be moved to modify their beliefs and conduct. Thus while this conception of political philosophy rejects the view that it is the task of philosophical argument to try to show that one set of political principles is necessarily morally preferable to another, it does not deny philosophy a role in such deliberations, nor does it deny that political philosophy may appropriately make a difference to our political ideas or practices. However, it will do so indirectly: it will not instruct us as to what we ought to believe, though it may show us that the implications of what we do think are not what we had taken them to be, or that our beliefs are contradictory, inconsistent, incoherent or otherwise confused.

Finally, logical and conceptual enquiry is not merely concerned with the meaning of words. Certainly most concepts can only be expressed and understood through words, but the same concept may be expressed in a variety of verbal formulations and the same word may be used to denote more than one concept. Concepts, especially complex political concepts such as freedom, authority, justice and such like, incorporate our understanding of the world and combine to form our beliefs and commitments. While sensitivity to language and appreciation of nuances of meaning is often important and helpful, few misunderstandings of philosophical enquiry are so pernicious as the claim that it is merely about the definition of words. The kind of conceptual enquiry which is fundamental to philosophy is not reducible to lexicography.

In sum, therefore, political philosophy understood as logical and conceptual enquiry is neither uncritical nor practically irrelevant. Nor is its concern with meaning that of the lexicographer. Political philosophy seeks to explore the values, beliefs and concepts in terms of which we understand and interpret our political experience. However, it is in the nature of the case that these values, beliefs and concepts lack the precision of those employed, for example, in physics and mathematics. There is, therefore, an inevitable *roughness* in the discussion of such concepts and values. Concepts such as democracy, justice, freedom, equality and political obligation cannot be characterised with the precision of natural numbers or scientific laws. In discussing political concepts, values and beliefs, and their presuppositions and implications, regular resort must be made to qualifying adjectives such as 'normally', 'commonly', 'frequently' and so on. Moreover, the interpretation of these concepts and values is also, to some extent, a matter of political dispute.

Both these considerations, therefore, set limits to what can be reasonably expected from political philosophy. It should help us to articulate and deepen our understanding of concepts and beliefs, and to clarify the issues at stake in assessing competing interpretations. However, it may not enable us to resolve some disputes or supply a precise and uncontroversial elucidation of basic political concepts and values. How far philosophical enquiry can take us is always an open question; yet we should also be conscious that political philosophy cannot be, for the most part at least, an exact science. Bearing this in mind, therefore, it is appropriate now to provide a rather fuller characterisation of the problem of political obligation.

Justifying political obligation

In the final section of this chapter I shall attempt to refine and elaborate the problem of political obligation, and briefly relate it to the preceding comments on political philosophy, by making a number of preliminary remarks about the nature of the problem as it is perceived within political philosophy. First, as I indicated earlier, the term 'political obligation' is not much used outside of philosophical discussion. For this reason, if no other, there could not be any ordinary language analysis of the term, for it is not in the relevant sense part of 'ordinary language'. Thus, the expression 'political obligation' is something of a term of art: a construct of political philosophers for identifying and relating to each other a range of issues concerned with the relations between individual and polity. While political philosophers have interpreted these issues in subtly different ways, traditionally there have been at least three questions which are central to philosophical discussions of political obligation. These are:

1. To whom or what do I have political obligations?

2. What are the extent and limits of these obligations?
3. What is the explanation or justification of these obligations?

While it is the first two questions which are usually most practically pressing, it is the third which is philosophically fundamental.

The first two questions largely presuppose an answer to the third, at least to the extent that they assume that we have some political obligations; whereas the third question is precisely about whether there are any such obligations at all, and if so what are their grounds or justification. This book focuses almost exclusively on this last question: how it has been interpreted; the answers that have been given to it; and the kind of answers which are appropriate. The second question will be largely ignored, though as I shall explain towards the end of the book it is doubtful if much which is illuminating can be said at a general level in answer to it. A partial answer to the first question is, as I shall explain shortly, implicit within the very conception of political obligation. Moreover, most philosophical accounts of the justification of political obligation also intimate answers to the first two questions. It is, therefore, the question of justification which has been taken to be the kernel of the philosophical problem of political obligation.

This leads to the second point which concerns the nature of the relationship between people and their political community, and the kind of justification of it which philosophers have sought to provide. Political obligation is understood to express a moral or ethical relationship between people and their political community. This claim is not entirely uncontroversial and has been denied by some philosophers (e.g. McPherson, 1967). I shall discuss and reject this denial in Chapter 6 but it is very much a maverick opinion and, for the most part, I shall simply assume its falsity. Political obligation concerns the moral or ethical bonds between individuals and their political community. To understand one's relationship to the political community of which one is a member in ethical terms is not to see it as simply involving submission to the arbitrary imposition of force; nor is it to see the relationship exclusively in terms of what one can get out of it or of how it serves one's own self-interest. Thus, for example, to conform to the requirements of one's polity only through fear of punishment if one does not, or because it happens to be beneficial to do so, is not to act on one's political obligations. While the dictates of prudence, self-interest and morality may coincide on occasion, on others they will not. As with other moral requirements, political obligation may require us to act in ways contrary to those which prudence or self-interest would suggest.

Moreover, though I shall mostly use the term 'political obligation' in discussing this moral relationship, such usage should not be taken as implying that this bond must be one of obligations rather than duties, as some philosophers have distinguished these terms (e.g. Brandt, 1965; Hart, 1967). No systematic distinction will be made between obligations and duties, but since nothing of substance in the subsequent argument depends upon a failure to observe this distinction it is not necessary to explore it further here. Both terms are used to indicate general moral reasons for acting, though of course neither indicates an *absolute* moral claim on our actions. Since, at the very least, obligations or duties can conflict with each other, to recognise an obligation is not necessarily to identify a *conclusive* reason for action. For instance, if I have promised to meet a friend at a particular time, I have an obligation to do so, but I ought not to act on that obligation if to do so would prevent me from taking a seriously sick child to hospital. This does not mean that obligations can be overridden as or when we like, but only that, at the very least, they can be overridden by other conflicting moral claims on us. Particular obligations, therefore, provide us with moral reasons for acting which are yet not 'all things considered' reasons. In deciding how to act on a particular occasion we have to take account of *all* the relevant reasons, which may mean that some obligations are overridden by others.

Thus to identify an action as being required by our political obligation is not to show that we must always perform it, though it is to indicate one (moral) reason which we have to so act. We must not forget that political obligations exist in a wider moral context, and are far from exhaustive of the moral claims which can be made on us. Political obligation involves the recognition that the political community has moral claims on its members, which generally provide weighty but not necessarily conclusive reasons for action: political obligation is about the obligations or duties concomitant on membership of a polity. Philosophers have understood their task to be one of explaining the nature of this moral relationship; more specifically this has most usually been interpreted as seeking a moral justification for the authority of government and the obligations of citizens. Again, this has usually been thought to require the deriving of political obligation from one or more general moral principles or locating it within some more comprehensive moral theory.

The third point to note is that the obligation is 'political'. In this context, what is meant by this claim is that the moral obligation has to do with a person's membership of a particular polity. It is linguistically unobjectionable to refer to membership of a political party or commitment to a cause as entailing or creating political obligations. However, these are not the obligations that the term generally denotes, and in what follows the use of 'political' in political obligation will refer exclusively to membership of a polity. For the most part I shall use the slightly unusual term 'polity', or the less forbidding 'political community' rather than 'state', so as not to prejudge the question of how far the arguments apply to other forms of polity such as the Greek *polis* or some tribal societies. However, states are certainly the most common and obvious examples of polities and most of the subsequent discussion is directed towards them without considering how far what is said applies to other forms of polity. It is not, though, an issue which should be resolved by definitional fiat. The key features of a polity, as understood here, are that it is the most comprehensive and inclusive structure of social organisation within a territory; that sovereign power is exercised by an authority, usually a government; and that its members are syst•matically related to each other through the terms of their membership. Many important questions could be raised about this brief characterisation of a polity, but it should provide sufficient guidance at this stage. Inevitably there will be borderline and disputed cases, but there are many which are not: Athens, Sparta and Rome were all polities, so today are the USA, Israel, Iran, India and Britain. These are all polities to which the issue of political obligation is relevant.

There is one further preliminary point which is especially important in relation to the subsequent discussion. This concerns the common assimilation of the problem of political obligation with the question of whether or not a person is obliged to obey the law. Such an assimilation, however, results in an inadequate characterisation of political obligation. The question of the grounds of an obligation to obey the law is open to two broad lines of interpretation, neither of which necessarily coincides precisely with the problem of political obligation. First, if the question is understood quite generally to be asking about reasons which would oblige us to obey any law then it is too broad, for it fails to focus with sufficient specificity on the particular relationship between persons and the political community of which they are members, which is essential to a distinctively political obligation. Reasons which justify obedience to law, independent of whether or not the law is that of the polity of which a person is a member, are not reasons which explain political obligation: they are not reasons which explain the particular relationship which characterises political obligation. This requirement that any adequate account of political obligation must concern the particular relationship between the polity and the members of that polity is what has become known as the 'particularity requirement' (Simmons, 1979, pp. 31–5). Political obligation is understood as the special moral relationship which obtains between members and *their* political community. Failure to appreciate this point effectively debars a theory from being an account of *political* obligation, whatever merits it may otherwise possess. Second, however, if the question is interpreted more narrowly to mean why is a person obliged to the law of his or her polity, then though this is part of the problem of political obligation, there may be other aspects to the problem which this interpretation does not encompass. Political obligation may include more than an obligation to obey the law of the polity of which one is a member. There may be other obligations or responsibilities specifically deriving from one's membership of a particular polity, which are not enshrined in the law and which if not observed do not incur a legal penalty. Moreover, as we shall see later, the relationship between political obligation and obedience to the law is more complex than simple reference to an obligation to obey the law may suggest.

There are, it need hardly be said, entirely legitimate and interesting enquiries into the nature of legal obligation and the moral claims of law, and it would be mistaken to deny that some of the issues and arguments are relevant to political obligation (see e.g. Carnes, 1960; Mackie, 1981; Pennock and Chapman, 1970; Smith, 1976; Wasserstrom, 1968). Unfortunately, however, failure to recognise that questions about political obligation are not necessarily identical with, or reducible to, questions about the obligation to obey the law – especially the failure to take account of the particularity requirement – has resulted in considerable confusion. In consequence, political philosophers have often been concerned with subtly but importantly different questions. In so far as this is the case there will necessarily be some mismatch between the concerns of those who equate the two sets of issues and the point of view adopted in this book. Hence, there is inevitably some movement between these viewpoints in the ensuing discussions, resulting in some shifts of focus and blurring of distinctions. This is a problem to which we shall have to return from time to time in subsequent chapters, though it is not easy to see how the messiness which this confusion sometimes entails can be altogether avoided. Nor, indeed, is such messiness uncommon in political philosophy.

The principal purpose of this chapter has been to introduce the problem of political obligation; to attempt a preliminary clarification of some of the issues to which it gives rise; and to indicate briefly the kind of enquiry to be undertaken in this book. In what follows I shall begin by considering critically some of the more philosophically resilient and influential accounts of political obligation. This task is undertaken in Chapters 2 to 4. My approach in these chapters is to distinguish different types of theories of political obligation, and to explore the strengths and weaknesses of these broad types. Any such approach, and especially one that attempts to cover a good deal of ground in brief compass, will have its limitations. In particular, it can prove somewhat procrustean both in its neglect of the richness and complexity of theories which largely fit within the classification, and in its treatment of those theories which escape such comfortable classification. In addition to these limitations, my accounts of earlier philosophers' ideas are often rather insensitive to their historical context. This in part reflects my desire to focus primarily on arguments which continue to have philosophical currency; a desire which also partly explains the relative neglect of some philosophers. However, in other cases, I must confess that this neglect is more the result of an inability to find a way to say anything very illuminating in the limited space in which they would have to be discussed. Hegel is one philosopher who falls into this latter category, though I am by no means entirely unsympathetic to his views (see Hegel, 1952). Hence it is important to treat these chapters as no more than introductions to the theories they discuss and criticise.

In Chapter 5 I consider and reject the claim that since there is, or can be, no convincing account of political obligation, this shows that ordinarily at least most people have no political obligations. Again, this chapter can hardly claim to offer a comprehensive review of anarchism, but its argument needs also to be read in the context of the succeeding chapters. In Chapter 6 I sketch an alternative account of political obligation, which I claim is more satisfactory than other theories. However, as is also explained, it offers a rather different kind of account of political obligation from those considered in the earlier chapters. I am of course greatly indebted to a large number of other philosophers, some of whose ideas are criticised elsewhere in the book. However, I do not believe that the account which I defend has been set out in quite the same way before; and my concern is to try to set that account out as clearly as possible, rather than to trace its philosophical lineage. This account, however, is only a sketch and stands in need of considerable further elaboration and defence. In the Conclusion I briefly return to questions about the nature of political philosophy, and attempt to provide some indication of the underlying approach which informs my account of political obligation. We begin, though, by considering perhaps the most popular type of theories of political obligation – those which I label 'voluntarist'.

2 Voluntarist Theories

This chapter offers a critical assessment of one class of accounts of political obligation. These accounts, following terminology which has become current in this context, are labelled 'voluntarist' (Pateman, 1985; Riley, 1973). Such theories have proved consistently appealing in the long history of discussions of political obligation, but especially so in the modern world to theorists of a broadly liberal persuasion. Central to these theories is the role they attribute to individual choice or decision, to some specific act of voluntary commitment, in explaining or justifying political obligation. Their essential and common feature is simply that they seek to explain political obligation in terms of some freely chosen undertaking through which persons morally bind themselves to their polity. It is through this act or undertaking that people are thought to acquire their political obligations. The precise form of this act or undertaking; the conditions which render it freely chosen; the nature of the relationship implied; the extent of the obligation incurred; and to whom or what the obligation is owed, are all variously articulated within differing voluntarist accounts. Often these differences are important and for some purposes may be more significant than the features that these accounts share. However, without denying or underestimating those differences, the discussion that follows is premised on the assumption that it is legitimate and instructive to treat such differences for the most part as variations within one broad class or category of argument.

Thus in general the ensuing discussion will be concerned with what is common to these accounts – the features they share – rather than with what differentiates them from one another. One advantage of this strategy is that it enables us to focus upon one logically distinct type of argument without becoming diverted by peripheral or secondary detail. Another advantage in considering one broad type of argument, rather than the complex ideas of particular political theorists, is that the latter often contain several logically distinct arguments which coexist in uneasy, ambiguous and sometimes even confused relation to each other. Locke would be a good example of a political philosopher who employs the notion of consent in his account of political obligation yet leaves it unclear precisely how much weight it is supposed to bear within the overall theory he articulates (Locke, 1967). However, this approach also has some limitations, principal among which is that it is inclined to drain the actual accounts offered by individual political theorists of their richness and imaginative complexity. Some simplification, though, if not desirable, is probably unavoidable. Thus the discussion here is directed towards one type of argument and its central features, and the ideas of particular political theorists only in so far as they employ this type of argument.

Voluntarism and political obligation

Voluntarist accounts, it has been suggested, explain or justify political obligation in terms of some freely chosen act or undertaking which morally binds a person to his or her polity. Most commonly the claim has been that the majority, if not all, individuals have political obligations in at least some polities, and that these are to be explained by reference to an individual's voluntary act of commitment. However, some political philosophers have used voluntarist arguments in a more radical way to subvert the claim that most people, either now or in the past, have, or have had, any obligations to their polity. They argue that voluntarist theories give a basically correct account of political obligation, but they conclude from this that the vast majority of people, both now and in the past, have no such obligations. Political obligation exists only when people have freely chosen membership of their polity, but since most people do not freely choose, they are not obligated (e.g. Pateman, 1985). Somewhat crudely, the distinction is between voluntarist accounts which purport to explain or justify a relationship which has actually obtained between many people and their polity, and those which claim that the requisite conditions for the proper ascription of political obligation have, as a matter of fact, at best only rarely existed. In short, both are voluntarist in that they agree that some voluntary undertaking must provide the justification for political obligation, but they disagree as to whether or not most people have made such an undertaking. This disagreement results from a dispute either about what the conditions are that have to be met for an undertaking to be genuinely voluntary, or about whether or not in fact the appropriate conditions of a voluntary undertaking have been met.

This distinction is not a sharp one at the margins, but it does reveal a real and significant gulf between differing voluntarist accounts of political obligation: a gulf which is often reflected, for example, in different judgements about whether or not people have political obligations in liberal democratic states. It also means that, to some extent, distinct criticisms are appropriate to voluntarist accounts divided on this basis. Though later in this chapter I will address specifically those theories which endorse voluntarism but which claim that the conditions for political obligation have rarely if ever been met, most of the discussion here is concerned with what those conditions are or should be, and whether they have obtained (at least in some polities for most people). With respect to this last point, I shall be particularly concerned to assess the claim that liberal democratic polities have so successfully incorporated the requirements of voluntarism that the ascription of political obligation to their citizens is justified within the terms of a voluntarist theory. My conclusion about this, and about voluntarist theories of political obligation more generally, will be sceptical.

First, however, more needs to be said about the structure and content of voluntarist accounts of political obligation. The most familiar of these accounts are those which deploy concepts such as a social contract, or express or tacit consent. The role of these concepts in voluntarist accounts is to provide the relevant connection between the individual and the polity which explains or justifies the claim that people have a political obligation to their particular polity. What makes these accounts voluntarist is that they all regard the political relations constituted by membership of a polity as in some way the result of voluntary, freely chosen undertakings by those so related. Where they differ, however, is in the specific accounts they give of how such relations are instituted. Thus political obligation is variously understood to arise from, for example, a contract between many individuals to establish a political community, or a contract between individuals and their government, or the express or tacit consent of individuals to the government or the constitution. While these do not exhaust the possibilities, they are indicative of the range of claims that are characteristically made by voluntarist theories. In brief, what they

assert is that no person has any political obligation unless he or she
has voluntarily bound him or her self to a particular polity.
Furthermore, in explaining how individuals come to acquire this
obligation, voluntarist theorists also attempt to explain the precise
substance of the obligation, its extent and to whom or what it is
owed. However, the answers given to these questions inevitably vary
with the specific details of different voluntarist accounts.

Thus, for example, Thomas Hobbes famously argued in his
Leviathan 'that life in a state of nature [i.e. without political
authority] would be solitary, poor, nasty, brutish and short'
(Hobbes, 1968, Ch. 13). In order to escape from this condition, he
claimed, we covenant (i.e. contract) with each other to give up our
natural right to whatever we want in return for the protection of an
all-powerful sovereign. We agree to obey the sovereign, who is not
himself a party to the contract, whatever he commands; subject only
to the residual right we each have to protect our own life when it is
directly threatened, whether that threat is from the sovereign or
some other person or persons from whom the sovereign is unable or
unwilling to protect us. In this way we both establish the authority
of the sovereign and simultaneously acquire the obligation to obey
him. However, not surprisingly, many subsequent thinkers have
doubted whether Hobbes' cure, the absolute authority of the
sovereign and the (almost) unlimited obligation of the subject, was
any better than the disease of the state of nature which it was
supposed to remedy. Thus later in the seventeenth century, in his
Second Treatise on 'Government, John Locke, though also making
the social contract central to his theory, argued for a more limited
political authority (Locke, 1967). He also afforded a prominent
place in his account of political obligation to the notion of consent.

Locke, like Hobbes before him, explained the origin of political
obligation in a contract made in a pre-political state of nature.
However, Locke's conception of the state of nature is considerably
more benign than that of Hobbes, and the process by which political
authority is instituted is more complicated. According to Locke,
political authority arose in two stages: first through a unanimous
contract to form political society, and then by a majority decision to
entrust a government with legislative, executive and judicial powers.
Throughout this process people retain their natural rights to life,
liberty and property: the purpose of forming a political society with
a government is to provide for the better protection and impartial

enforcement of these rights than is possible in the state of nature. There, in the absence of any authoritative interpretation of these rights and any impartial body charged with their protection, there is inevitably some arbitrariness of judgement and erratic unpredictability of enforcement. Subsequent generations, not party to the original contract, acquire their political obligations through their consent: either in the form of an explicit oath of allegiance or through what Locke calls their 'tacit' consent. Locke is rather unclear about what is necessary for tacit consent, but it includes enjoying or making use of any property under the jurisdiction and protection of the state. The problems involved in the idea of consent, whether express or tacit, will provide a major focus of discussion later in this chapter and, therefore, will not be pursued further at this point.

The most important feature of Locke's account of political obligation, in contrast to that of Hobbes, is that it allowed for a right of resistance to an incompetent or tyrannical government; though how and by whom this was to be judged was again left somewhat unclear. It also gives rise to doubts about the real importance of consent within Locke's theory, for it sometimes seems that the significant question for political obligation becomes not whether a person consents, but whether the government is acting justly (Dunn, 1967). Indeed we can see Locke as embracing two different kinds of justification of political obligation: those which focus on the activities or moral qualities of the state and those which look to some voluntary act of commitment on the part of the citizen. It is only the latter which will be considered in this chapter.

Hobbes and Locke are undoubtedly two of the most important voluntarist theorists, but voluntarist theories of one kind or another have a long and complex history with roots dating back at least as far as classical Athens. In the *Crito,* Socrates considers escaping from his imprisonment and avoiding the death penalty but argues that the Laws (the embodiment of political authority in Athens) could legitimately ask of him: 'Are we or are we not speaking the truth when we say that you have undertaken, in deed if not in word, to live your life as a citizen in obedience to us? . . . It is a fact then that you are breaking covenants and undertakings made with us, although you made them under no compulsion or misunderstanding' (Plato, 1969, p. 93). Here is clearly expressed the thought that Socrates has, through his voluntary actions, entered into a covenant or agreement with the Laws of Athens, and has thereby acquired an obligation to obey them. Though this is not the only, or the most important, line of argument advanced in the *Crito*, it is a significant voluntarist strand in the broader position Socrates elaborates (see Woozley, 1979). Furthermore, elements of voluntarist theories have been detected in other Greek thinkers and in Roman Law as well as in Hooker, Grotius and Milton, before what is generally considered to be their full flowering in the work of Hobbes and Locke in the seventeenth century.

It would be implausible, therefore, to claim that voluntarist theories of political obligation are only articulated within a very historically specific set of socio-economic conditions. This is not to deny, however, that particular historical circumstances may favour, or be especially conducive to, their development. For example, it seems likely that the prominence of voluntarist theories in the seventeenth century owes a good deal to the peculiar social, economic and ideological changes that Europe was then undergoing; in particular, those consequent on the Reformation, the rise of Protestantism, and the emergence of market capitalism (Mac-Pherson, 1962). These circumstances did much to undermine the theory of the divine right of kings which had helped to justify the political authority of secular rulers during the period of the increasing separation of church and state. This theory, which perhaps receives its most articulate statement in the writings of Sir Robert Filmer, maintained that the authority of secular rulers had been directly ordained by God, and that therefore their subjects were morally obligated to obey the ruler's commands (Filmer, 1991). The theories of Hobbes and Locke, in their different ways, were both conscious attempts to develop a justification of political authority more suited to the changing historical conditions. Indeed, though I shall not attempt it here, an exploration of the historical context of seventeenth-century contract and consent theories can be especially illuminating about some of the merits and limitations of such theorising (Herzog, 1989). It is also possible to conjecture more generally that voluntarism is likely to prove particularly attractive when established authority is under attack, or where there is no settled moral consensus to which appeal can be made. However, whatever the merits of such a speculation, there can be no doubt that voluntarist theories have a venerable history (Gough, 1967; Lessnoff, 1986). Moreover, in one form or another, they continue to have a considerable attraction for political theorists: an appeal undiminished in our own time, as is illustrated in the work of several liberal political philosophers (Beran, 1977, 1987; Plamenatz, 1968; Tussman, 1960).

It is appropriate, therefore, briefly to consider what it is about voluntarist theories of political obligation which accounts for their persistent and continuing attractiveness. Why have political philosophers shown such remarkable tenacity and ingenuity in trying to reconstruct or rehabilitate such theories, despite what appear to be, as we shall shortly see, some fairly obvious and deep-rooted objections to them? These attractions have both a moral and philosophical dimension. Perhaps the principal feature of voluntarist theories which accounts for their appeal is the crucial role they assign to people's voluntary choices or commitments. For what obligates a person is some act (a contract, a promise, a form of words, or an action or actions expressing or implying consent) which is freely and voluntarily performed by that person. The individual is recognised as a morally free agent, only legitimately bound by the demands of the polity because of a free and voluntary undertaking to be so bound. Since the individual is the author of his or her own obligation, such an obligation in no way impairs the moral autonomy of the person. The lucid summary of the attractions of consent theory by A. J. Simmons serves equally for any voluntarist theory:

> '[It] respects our belief that the course a man's life takes should be determined, as much as possible, by his own decisions and actions. Since being born into a political community is neither an act we perform, nor the result of a decision we have made, we feel that this should not limit our freedom by automatically binding us to the government of that community. And these convictions serve as the basis of a theory of political obligation which holds that only the voluntary giving of a clear sign that one finds the state acceptable (and is willing to assume political bonds to it), can ever obligate one to support or comply with the commands of that state's government' (Simmons, 1979, p. 69).

On this view, the polity is an association of individuals much like other voluntary associations, such as sports clubs, political parties and trades unions, created and maintained by the freely entered into commitments of the multiplicity of individuals who compose them. In the modern world, at least, the voluntary membership of an association is usually thought of as a necessary condition of its having authority over its members and correspondingly of their acquiring obligations to it. If this is true of other associations, then why not of the polity? Clearly, if some account of political obligation along these lines were plausible, it would satisfy a widely held conviction that the moral authority of a polity resides in the voluntary agreement of its members, a conviction which is especially attractive to those of a broadly liberal political persuasion. Such an account would also have the benefit of rendering political obligation intelligible in terms which, if not transparent to the understanding, would at least identify it as belonging to that familiar category of moral obligations of which promises are paradigmatic. Hence if it were possible to formulate a convincing voluntarist account of political obligation, it would have considerable moral and philoso- phical appeal. What then are the objections to such an account? Is it possible to formulate a convincing voluntarist theory?

The most fundamental and obvious difficulty that has continually confronted voluntarist theories has been to discover anything that could reasonably be interpreted as corresponding to the type of act required to create a political obligation. We have a good idea, for example, of what acts are required to become a member of a club, but what comparable act is there which creates membership of a polity? Indeed, for those voluntarist theorists who claim to give an explanation or justification of political obligation in any existing polities, this problem appears insurmountable. This perhaps banal and obvious point is no less important for its familiarity and simplicity. In the case of a supposed contract the embarrassing questions to which this objection gives rise are easily apparent. When was this contract made? Who are the parties to the contract? What are the terms of the contract? Where are we to look to resolve any disputes about the contract? It does not seem that any social contract theory of this very simple form could possibly provide remotely plausible answers to most of these questions. It is true that in some times and places oaths of allegiance and declarations of loyalty have been common, but how plausible is it to regard these as meeting the conditions of a contractual basis for political obliga- tion? First, even if they are thought to fit the bill, this would only explain the political obligation of those who had entered into such commitments. Second, such oaths and declarations would need to have been freely entered into if they were to count as genuine contracts. This is a point which will be developed more fully later when considering the conditions that the weaker notion of consent requires to be met, if an act or utterance is to count as a genuine expression of voluntary agreement. Thirdly, the content of these oaths and declarations is often either too vague or too narrow to license a general political obligation. Finally, such oaths and declarations lack features which are usual to contracts: for example, only one party undertakes an obligation with the other offering little in return.

However, these objections might give rise to the reply that they take the idea of contract far too literally. Perhaps a more informal analogue of a contract such as a promise, bargain or agreement is involved. Indeed, it might be argued that what such oaths and declarations, as well as other acts, should be understood as expressing is rather a person's consent to the authority of the government. Thus, since it seems likely that the concept of consent will prove to be more defensible than that of the more formal contract, subsequent criticism will be directed to voluntarist accounts which focus upon consent. Any criticisms of consent theories are likely to apply *mutatis mutandis* to all genuinely voluntarist contract accounts (though, as will be explained later, there are versions of contract theory which are not genuinely voluntarist, as defined here). It is, therefore, most profitable to concentrate on consent theories as the most plausible and sophisticated of voluntarist accounts of political obligation.

Consent

Consent, it has been suggested, is a more informal and less legalistic concept than contract. We give and refuse consent in a wide range of contexts, for a multiplicity of purposes and in a variety of forms: a patient consents to a surgical operation; a woman consents to allow a friend to borrow her car; a father consents to the marriage of his 17-year-old daughter; an employer consents to her employee taking the day off; a famous author consents to the use of his name in a charitable cause; homosexual acts are legal in Britain if performed in private by consenting adults; and so on. However, it would be a mistake to infer from this variety that there are not reasonably precise conditions that an act or utterance must meet if it is legitimately to be understood as a genuine expression of consent. Richard Flathman has usefully identified three such requirements. On his account a person must, when the appropriate background conditions of freedom of choice obtain:

a.   know what he consents to;
b.   intend to consent to it;
c.   communicate his knowledge of what he is consenting to and his intention to consent (that is, communicate his consent) to the person or persons to whom the consent is given (Flathman, 1972, p. 220).

These seem reasonable conditions to require of an action or utterance if it is to be legitimately interpreted as an expression of consent, in anything like our ordinary understanding of the term. These requirements will subsequently be referred to respectively as the 'knowledge', 'intention' and 'communication' conditions. However, there are some preliminary observations on these conditions which need to be made.

First, the knowledge condition, which requires that a person know what it is that he or she consents to, is more complex than it might appear. For sometimes, due to what is called the opacity of belief or knowledge, it can be reasonably claimed that a person consented to something even though he or she did not know or fully understand what had been consented to. For example, if a mother consents to her young son going to the theatre one evening she may also consent to his coming home late. This may be true even though the mother did not know she was consenting to her son's coming home late, perhaps because she mistakenly thought the play finished earlier. (Of course, the implications would be different if her son had misled her about the time at which the performance finished.) Thus the 'knowledge condition' must not be interpreted in too narrow or strict a way, though it is obvious, despite this indeterminacy in its application, that it is an indispensable condition in deciding whether or not, in any particular case, consent has been given. Indeed, and this is the second point, it should be noted that, despite the apparent clarity of the three conditions, it is in practice sometimes very difficult to be confident about whether or not they have been met.

It is sometimes as a matter of fact very difficult to determine whether or to what a person has consented. Sexual intercourse and some kinds of medical situation provide two notorious contexts in which the difficulty of establishing whether or not consent has been given may be considerable. Of course such difficulties do not preclude there being many instances in which the presence or absence of consent is clear and entirely unproblematic. The third observation is that all three conditions apply equally to tacit consent as to express or explicit consent. Since this point is more controversial, and it is highly relevant to what may seem to be the most plausible version of consent theory, it is worth considering more fully.

The notion of tacit consent is principally familiar from situations in which an individual on being given an opportunity to express dissent from some policy, proposal or other course of action does not do so and remains silent or impassive. Here it would often be natural to say that, though the individual does not do or say anything in response to the proposal, he or she tacitly consents to it. Such situations are especially familiar in committee meetings though they also exist in more informal and less structured settings. For example, in getting into a taxi and stating my destination, though no mention is made of a fare, I normally tacitly agree to pay the fare. What distinguishes tacit from express or explicit consent, in this as in other instances, is only the *manner* or *form* in which it is indicated. Tacit consent is expressed through silence or passivity. However, it is obvious that not just any instance of passivity or silence can reasonably be interpreted as an act of consent, or else each of us would be consenting to all manner of things all the time.

What singles out a particular instance of silence or passivity as an act of consent is precisely those conditions Flathman identifies. The person must know what it is he or she is consenting to, subject to the qualification mentioned earlier; must intend to give consent; and most importantly in this context must know that silence or passivity will be understood as an expression or sign of consent. These conditions need not imply any sustained or complicated process of explicit reasoning on the part of the person consenting, but it is only when they are met that it is appropriate to impute tacit consent to someone. Thus tacit consent is distinctive only in the form in which it is expressed and in other respects is essentially similar to express consent. In particular it is important to emphasise that the qualification of consent by the adjective 'tacit' does not imply a radically different type of consent, logically distinct from other forms of consent. In the end this is to say no more than that tacit consent is an instance of *consent*, but to say that much may prevent one being misled when the emphasis is placed upon its being *tacit* consent. The difference between tacit and express consent is of the same order as the difference between consent being indicated by raising a hand or by saying yes. The nature of silence and passivity may make such consent more difficult to identify and more disputable in practice, but the logic of tacit consent is no different from that of express consent.

The intention, knowledge and communication conditions are all necessary but not sufficient conditions for an act counting as a genuine expression of consent. There also have to be present what were earlier referred to as the appropriate background conditions of choice. These need to be explained more fully, though they are both more vague and more controversial than the other conditions. However, their necessity can easily be shown from the following example. If presented with a choice between his money or his life, a man cannot be said to have genuinely consented to the taking of his money, even though he allows it to be taken and the intention, knowledge and communication conditions have all been met. The reason for denying that genuine consent is involved in this example is that the man did not have the appropriate kind of choice as to whether or not to refuse his consent. It would be natural to say that he had no real alternative to consenting, though it would not be literally true to say that he had *no* choice at all. The problem here is in establishing how much, or, better, what sort of choice is necessary for an expression of consent to be genuine. This is particularly important for voluntarist theorists of political obligation, who need to show that people do have a real choice if consent is to play the role required by their theories.

Matters are further complicated, however, if we consider a rather different example. If a man is faced with a choice between a serious operation to save his life and the inevitable consequences of a terminal illness, it would be quite proper, if he agrees to the operation, to say that he gave his consent. Indeed, under normal circumstances his consent is just what is required before the operation can be performed. In both this example and that of the man faced with the choice between his money and his life the man will die unless he gives his consent to one course of action, yet in the latter example the attribution of consent is strongly counter-intuitive, while in the medical example it would seem to be unexceptional. How, then, are these cases to be distinguished? Why is one properly understood as an expression of consent and the other not?

The different responses to these two examples is best explained in normative terms. The difference cannot be satisfactorily accounted for simply in terms of the number of choices available or in terms of their attractiveness, though in some instances these may be relevant considerations. In the two examples under discussion, if they are filled out in appropriate detail, both the number of choices and their utilities or values could be equivalent, yet the difference in judgement about whether or not consent had been given would persist. The normative feature of these two examples which most plausibly explains this difference of response is the presence or absence of coercion by another person or persons. In the first example it is the clearly coercive element of the threat that invalidates the imputation of consent, whereas in the medical example no coercion is either exercised or threatened.

Unfortunately, though this distinction between the presence or absence of coercion is easily observed in these particular examples, it is, in many circumstances, notoriously a matter of vigorous dispute as to what is to count as an instance of coercion. For example, when are the unpleasant consequences of an action to be understood as simply following from the action and when as coercively induced? When does persuasion become coercion? The point is not that answers cannot be given to these questions but that such answers will often be both lacking in precision and also controversial and disputed. Many cases will be clear, such as in the two examples cited, but some of the most interesting and important in political contexts are likely to be contested. For example, labour contracts within a capitalist economic system are characteristically viewed as coercive exchanges by Marxists while defenders of the free-market typically see them as paradigmatic instances of free exchange. Similar disputes are liable to pervade discussions of consent in the context of voluntarist theories of political obligation. For example, Hobbes argued that even contracts entered into under extreme duress, such as those made by people whose lives were directly threatened by an external aggressor, were no less voluntary and hence equally obligatory as those made under much more auspicious circumstances (Hobbes, 1968, Ch. 20). While this view has some justification within Hobbes' metaphysical system, it has not won much favour with other philosophers, and generally it has not been thought to meet the conditions of an authentically voluntarist theory of political obligation. However, even among those who accept that the background conditions of choice require that genuine consent must not be coercively induced, there is still an important area of disagreement as to what exactly is to count as the absence of coercion. Any account of consent needs to be sensitive to these difficulties.

It may also be appropriate at this point to advert briefly to one further area of contention. This concerns the claims of some feminist theorists, who have argued that the way in which the notion of consent is characteristically employed within the theories of political philosophers, and indeed the entire social contract tradition, is riddled by patriarchal assumptions (Pateman, 1988, 1989). These assumptions have been such as effectively to exclude women from consent or participation in the social contract; for either it has been tacitly implied that the relevant parties are male heads of households or, as with Rousseau, it has been explicitly stated that women are excluded for other reasons. Historically there can be no doubt that there is much justice in the feminist complaint. The more difficult and more philosophically interesting question, however, concerns the extent to which this patriarchal bias is inherent within voluntarism. If it were, then this would constitute a compelling objection to the entire enterprise of developing a voluntarist theory of political obligation. Fortunately, at least for those committed to this project, there is no reason to think that this is the case. It is probably true that in some contexts implicitly patriarchal assumptions have helped the whole idea of a social contract appear more practicable, but there does not seem to be anything in the logic of voluntarism which *necessitates* a patriarchal bias. Thus while the relationship between various voluntarist theories of political obligation and patriarchalism is a topic worthy of further exploration, such theories are not irredeemably compromised by this historical association. There is no apparent reason why such theories cannot be reconstructed along non-patriarchal lines, as indeed I have done in this chapter. It remains then to consider whether there are other reasons for rejecting an account of political obligation in terms of consent.

Political obligation and consent

The central problem for consent theorists, as with all voluntarist theories, has been to discover any action in the personal history of most individuals which meets the conditions necessary for the ascription of political obligation; that is, to discover any act registering the appropriate consent. Who has consented? When and how have they consented? To what have they consented? To whom have they given their consent? Though many very different answers to these questions could be and have been offered, two interpretations of tacit consent have proved especially popular among consent theorists. First, it has been claimed that continued residence within a polity, or the enjoyment of the benefits consequent upon continued residence, provides sufficient evidence that an individual consents to its political arrangements. Though the two formulations of this interpretation are not strictly equivalent, and the expression 'political arrangements' for indicating what is consented to is deliberately vague, the differences which are blurred by this general formulation can be safely ignored for present purposes; for the objections which follow apply irrespective of these differences. The second interpretation of tacit consent is of more recent provenance and involves the claim that voting in a genuinely democratic election is an expression of consent to the authority of the duly elected government. This suggestion is obviously much more restricted in its scope, being limited to polities which have authentically democratic constitutional and political practices. Here it should be noted that there is likely to be some dispute about what constitutes a genuinely democratic election and also about whether any, and if so what, limits are implied upon what a government may legitimately do. Again so far as possible the details of these disputes will be ignored. I shall begin by considering the first interpretation of tacit consent.

Does the claim that residence, or the enjoyment of the benefits of residence, implies consent meet the conditions necessary for an act to count as an expression of consent? It seems highly implausible to think that it does. There are no commonly understood conventions by reference to which continued residence or the enjoyment of its fruits can be reasonably interpreted as implying consent. It is not at all clear what individuals are consenting to, that they know they are consenting, or that they intend to do so. There may of course be other arguments, for example from fairness, justice, gratitude or utility, as to why individuals *should* consent but these are not to the point here. The question is rather whether people through such actions *do* imply their consent and to this the answer must be no.

Additionally there is further reason why residence or the benefits of residence are likely to be thought dubious candidates as genuine indications of consent. It might reasonably be doubted in many instances whether the background conditions of choice obtain. In many circumstances there is simply no realistic alternative to continued residence. Many polities do not permit emigration or radically constrain it, and even when it is neither legally proscribed nor actively discouraged it is often likely to be a prohibitively costly option. For as David Hume wrote in a frequently cited passage:

'Can we seriously say, that a poor peasant or artisan has a free choice to leave his country, when he knows no foreign language or manners, and lives, from day to day, by the small wages which he acquires? We may as well assert that a man, by remaining in a vessel, freely consents to the domination of the master; though he was carried on board while asleep, and must leap into the ocean and perish, the moment he leaves her' (Hume, 1953, p. 51).

Even allowing for Hume's characteristic rhetorical flourish, there is surely much force to his observation. It is still more telling when, even for those to whom emigration might be a real possibility, the choice they face may only be between polities more or less like their own (and in any case in the modern world immigration is yet more tightly controlled than emigration). There is no longer any refuge for a person who wants to escape political relations entirely, and hence the choice facing such a person will be more apparent than real. Together these considerations comprise a powerful case against mere residence, or the enjoyment of the fruits of residence, being regarded as indications of consent. The nature of the acts involved are insufficiently voluntary; their connection to the political obligation to which they are supposed to give rise is too diffuse and indeterminate; and there are no generally accepted conventions by reference to which it can be reasonably argued that the 'knowledge', 'intention' and 'communication' conditions have been met.

It may be that we could conceive of political arrangements being so changed that many, and perhaps all, of these objections would no longer have any force, and this is a possibility which is explored with some ingenuity by Harry Beran (Beran, 1987). He advances what he calls a membership version of consent theory according to which 'consent consists in accepting membership of the state' and this requires peoples' actual personal consent (Beran, 1987, Ch. 3). His is a reform theory in that he thinks no existing states meet the conditions for such consent, but where his account is unusual is in his claim that such reforms as are necessary are comparatively modest, and that 'consent-based political authority and obligation is possible without utopian changes to existing liberal democracies' (Beran, 1987, p. 153). In particular he argues that people should be given a formal opportunity on reaching maturity to accept membership of the state, or there should be some clearly established convention according to which continued residence (or perhaps the assumption of the rights of citizenship) will be generally understood to indicate consent. Furthermore, if the proportion of people living within a state who are under consent-based political obligations is to be maximised then the following conditions should obtain:

a. there is a legal right to emigrate and to change one's nationality
b. secession is constitutionally permitted if desired and feasible
c. a dissenters' territory is created (Beran, 1987, p. 125).

While such conditions would not necessarily establish that everyone within a state consented – there might still be a role for a status similar to resident alien – they would be sufficient to establish the political obligation of most people. How successful then is Beran's reformist, membership version of consent theory in meeting our earlier objections?

Certainly the kind of changes to the liberal democratic state that Beran recommends would do something to make it more of a 'voluntary association' in accordance with the requirements of a genuinely voluntarist consent theory. However, there remain several problems. First, it seems doubtful whether these proposed reforms really are as modest as Beran thinks. For example, both the theory of secession and even more the idea of dissenters' territories (places where those who do not consent can move) are full of difficulties. While Beran has tried to deal with some of the problems of secession, he has almost nothing to say about dissenters' territories. It seems quite bizarre to think that a dissenters' territory whose occupants may only be united by their refusal to consent to the state, represents a viable option, let alone one which is likely to attract many dissenters. Second, even if liberal democratic states were reconstructed along the lines Beran describes would that be sufficient to make membership of the state voluntary? Beran concedes that the choices available would be limited but he denies that this limitation is in any way coercive. However, this is to be insufficiently attentive to the extent to which the choices available to a person are structured by the state. This need not be a problem if one already accepts the authority of the state over such matters, but since that authority is precisely what consent is supposed to establish this seems to beg the important question. For the person who does not consent and therefore does not recognise its authority, the state is behaving coercively in so restricting the options. Nor is this only a problem for the non-consenter, since many people may consent who would not otherwise do so, if they were offered a different range of options. Since on Beran's account 'the state is not a naturally occurring phenomenon' (Beran, 1987, p. 149), the question at least arises as to why the range of choices with which the state confronts us provides an appropriate situation for deciding whether or not to consent to its authority. Thus I suggest that for all its ingenuity Beran's attempt to re-establish the credentials of consent theory is less than successful.

Does, then, the second interpretation of tacit consent – that of voting in a democratic election – fare any better? It might seem to, for as John Plamenatz writes:

'Where there is an established process of election to an office, then, *provided the election is free*, anyone who takes part in the process consents to the authority of whoever is elected to the office. This, I think, is not to ascribe a new meaning to the word *consent* but is only to define a very ordinary, and important political use of it. The citizen who votes at an election is presumed to understand the significance of what he is doing, and if the election is free, he has voluntarily taken part in a process which confers authority on someone who otherwise would not have it' (Plamenatz, 1968, p. 170).

As Plamenatz himself agrees, it is no doubt a difficult task to specify precisely those conditions which make an election free but some latitude should be allowed on this matter; though it should perhaps be remarked that radical critics of liberal democracy have argued that elections within liberal democracies do not meet the required conditions. Sometimes, taking a lead from Rousseau, they have maintained that only direct participatory democracies would meet the conditions for consent (Rousseau, 1973; Pateman, 1985). However, leaving aside this line of argument, on Plamenatz's own account we should presumably have to exclude not only elections in Eastern Europe (at least until very recently) and much of Africa but also those in countries such as Australia, where voting is legally compulsory. This last exclusion might itself make us sceptical of Plamenatz's contention, for it seems odd to think that the legal compulsion to vote makes such a fundamental difference to the political obligation of the citizens of Australia and, say, the USA, where voting is entirely optional, as his account must imply. However, there are also more serious objections.

First, there is the obvious point, that on this account only those who vote can be said to consent to the authority of the duly elected government. This will as a matter of fact leave a large minority, and in some cases a majority, of the citizens of any existing state which could reasonably be thought to have free elections without any political obligations. The attempt to claim, as some have, that abstainers in such elections have also given their consent, is so wildly implausible as not to merit serious consideration. If both voting and not voting are interpreted as expressions of consent then it is obvious that consent cannot be distinguished from refusal to consent: if it is impossible not to consent then consent cannot seriously be regarded as voluntary. This is recognised, for example, by Tussman who concedes that many ' "citizens" have in no meaningful sense agreed to anything'. They are like 'political child-brides who have a status they do not understand and which they have not acquired by their own consent', and such 'non-consenting adult citizens are, in effect, like minors who are governed without their own consent' (Tussman, 1960, pp. 36–7). At the very least, if voting is to be a genuine expression of a person's consent, then that person must vote.

Secondly, Plamenatz's account of what is involved in or implied by a democratic election is open to dispute. Some people participate in elections in an entirely pragmatic or instrumental spirit and do not regard themselves or others as *morally* bound by the result.

Though we might have a different attitude it is not clear that there is any logical or conceptual mistake in denying that voters are morally bound to recognise the authority of whoever wins the election. The reason for this relates to a general failing in Plamenatz's account which is that elections may be understood simply as mechanisms for deciding who will rule rather than conferring authority on those who are elected. The former need not imply the latter, nor is there anything intrinsic to democratic elections which compels anyone who participates in them to adopt the latter understanding of them. For example, an anarchist who denies authority to any government, may vote in an election, believing some governments to be worse than others, in an attempt to ensure that the least bad government is elected. The decision about voting may be based on a pragmatic judgement about what is for the best in the circumstances without any belief that the election secures the authority of the government or entails any obligation towards it. It is simply not true, therefore, that participation in an election necessarily either expresses or implies consent to the authority of whoever is elected. Of course some people do believe that being democratically elected is what confers authority on a government and for them voting in an election may entail a political obligation, but the point is that this belief cannot be inferred merely from someone's participation in a democratic election. It is this illegitimate inference which underlies Plamenatz's account of democratic elections as expressing or implying consent on the part of those who participate in them.

The conclusion of the argument so far is that voluntarist theories, to the extent that they attempt to provide an account of political obligation in existing or previously existing polities, generally fail. The principal reason for this failure is that no such theory can give a satisfactory account of the undertaking that supposedly generates the obligation. Whether it be contract, express or tacit consent that is said to be the basis of political obligation, there is no warrant for these claims in the personal history of most people. Participation in democratic institutions and some oaths of allegiance, provided they are voluntary and have the appropriate content, may do something to explain the political obligations of some citizens. However, the numbers involved are likely to be small and the obligations incurred highly circumscribed. At best, therefore, consent theory may have a limited role to play in explaining the genesis of some specific political obligations for some people. These considerations, however, might be thought to be less than compelling because they treat voluntarist theories of political obligation too literally. Thus, it might be claimed that they miss the point of such theories because they treat them with inappropriate naïveté. Not surprisingly, my argument will be that they do not, and indeed it will be further suggested that it is only by transforming voluntarist theories into a logically different kind of account of political obligation that these objections can be circumvented. In order to show this we must examine some other interpretations of consent theory.

First, it should be noted that in discussing consent theory it was simply assumed, without argument, that consent must mean straightforward 'personal consent'. A. J. Simmons distinguishes theories of personal consent, defined as those where 'political obligations are grounded in the personal consent of each citizen who is bound', from both 'historical consent' and 'majority consent' theories (Simmons, 1979, pp. 60–1, 71–4). The 'historical consent' theory holds 'that the political obligations of all citizens (of all times) within a state are generated by the consent of the members of the *first* generation of the political community' (Simmons, 1979, p. 60). As Simmons observes, this theory has little to commend it and it can be briskly dismissed. There is no reason to think that any actual states were in fact created by the initial consent of the members of the first generation. Moreover, it is only in special circumstances, such as where one person is authorised to act on behalf of another, circumstances which clearly do not obtain in this case, that the act of one individual can morally bind another. Finally, even if those circumstances did obtain, the 'historical consent' theory could not be regarded as a genuinely voluntarist account of political obligation, for all later generations would have no choice whether or not to be so bound. So much then for historical consent.

The 'majority consent' theory, on the other hand, claims that citizens are all obligated to their polity when a majority of their number consent to it. This theory too is vulnerable to compelling objections and need not detain us for long. First, it is clearly parasitic upon the theory of 'personal consent', since a majority must personally consent and this has already been found to be an untenable claim. Second, it is necessary to give some account of how a majority, could morally bind a minority who have not consented and it is not easy to see how this is to be done. Third, supposing that some such account is offered, the 'majority consent' theory could not be regarded as a fully voluntarist account of political obligation since it would entail that the minority could be morally bound without their consent, and even against their will. The second and third objections could be met if there were some prior agreement of all to be bound by majority decisions, but then this prior agreement would itself be subject to the same objections as those made earlier to personal consent theories. Thus neither the doctrine of 'historical consent' nor that of 'majority consent' looks remotely attractive as an alternative to 'personal consent'. Indeed both theories are either parasitic upon 'personal consent', and hence open to the same objections as 'personal consent' theories, or are not genuinely voluntarist at all.

A rather different strategy which has been adopted in reconstructing consent or contract theories is to claim that such concepts should be understood as logical constructs. Such an approach is to be found, for example, in the contractarianism of Kant (Kant, 1991). One recent version of it is that of Hanna Pitkin, who writes:

> '[Y]our personal consent is essentially irrelevant to your obligation to obey, or its absence. Your obligation to obey depends upon the character of the government – whether it is acting within the bounds of *the* (only possible) contract . . . So, not only is your personal consent irrelevant, but it actually no longer matters whether this government or any government was really founded by a group of men deciding to leave the state of nature by means of a contract. As long as a government's actions are within the bounds of what such a contract hypothetically *would have* provided, would have *had* to provide, those living within its territory must obey. This is the true significance of what we have all learned to say in political theory: that the historical accuracy of the contract doctrine is basically irrelevant – that the contract is a logical construct. The only "consent" that is relevant is the hypothetical consent imputed to hypothetical, timeless, abstract, rational men' (Pitkin, 1972, p. 57).

Pitkin recognises that this reconstruction involves some transformation in the usual understanding of consent, but she still claims that her doctrine of 'hypothetical consent' can legitimately be understood as a version of consent theory. She writes:

'In one sense this "nature of the government" theory is thus a substitute for the doctrine of consent. But it may also be regarded as a new interpretation of consent theory, what we may call the doctrine of *hypothetical* consent. For a legitimate government, a true authority, one whose subjects are obligated to obey it, emerges as being one to which they *ought to consent*, quite apart from whether they have done so. Legitimate government acts within the limits of the authority rational men would, abstractly and hypothetically, have to give a government they are founding. Legitimate government is government which *deserves* consent' (Pitkin, 1972, p. 62).

Whatever the merits of the substance of Pitkin's theory of 'hypothetical consent', and these will be considered in Chapter 4, it is potentially misleading to present it in the language of consent: the kind of account she presents is very different from that of voluntarist theories. There is one sense of hypothetical consent, however, which does conform more closely to the logic of voluntarist theories – where consent would *as a matter of fact* have been given but for some reason was not – but such cases are quite unusual and have little bearing on the problem of political obligation. They are considered more fully in Chapter 4 in the context of a more extended discussion of Pitkin's arguments.

At the risk of labouring the point, the mere word 'consent' is not the issue but rather the confusion that is created when it is used to cover logically different types of argument. The logic of 'hypothetical consent' is quite different from that of personal or actual consent, and arguments from hypothetical consent direct our attention to entirely different sorts of considerations. While actual consent theories require us to investigate the personal history of individuals to establish whether or not they have consented, and not, for example, whether it would have been wise or right for them to do so; hypothetical consent theories direct our attention to the reasons why it would be reasonable or rational for an individual to consent, whether or not any individual has in fact consented. In short, the doctrine of 'hypothetical consent' is not a voluntarist theory of political obligation at all and is more properly presented as a logically different type of theory. Furthermore, similar arguments would show that the same is true of various games-theoretical interpretations of social contract theory (see Taylor, 1976). Of course, to say this is not to show such accounts to be mistaken; only to identify them as not being genuinely voluntarist in character.

The limits of voluntarism

The argument so far has been that voluntarist accounts suffer from crippling defects when they purport to explain or justify political obligation within any known polities. In addition it has been suggested that attempts to reformulate these accounts to avoid the defects fail in one or both of two ways. Either the objections are only apparently avoided, usually through some conceptual obscurity, or the objections are genuinely avoided, but only by subverting the essentially voluntarist nature of the account and transforming it into a logically different type of theory. However, it may be interesting to consider in a rather more speculative and tentative spirit some of the background assumptions and beliefs that inform voluntarist accounts of political obligation. These reflections will also apply to those radical voluntarist theories which claim that the conditions for the justified ascription of political obligation (to more than a few individuals at best) have yet to be historically realised. In particular, three issues will be considered. First, there is the basic assumption that political obligation must be the result of a voluntary undertaking. Second, there is the underlying model of a polity as a voluntary association. Finally, there is the conception of the person implied by voluntarist theories.

Voluntarist accounts claim that political obligation is generated by some voluntary act, the performance of which creates the obligation for the person who so acts. Proponents of such accounts often seem attracted by Hobbes' assertion that there is no 'Obligation on any man, which ariseth not from some Act of his own' (Hobbes, 1968, p. 268). Michael Walzer seems to hold a similar view, for after quoting Hobbes and explaining his own adherence to consent theory, he writes: 'Nor do I want to offer a theoretical defence of the proposition that obligations derive only from consent. I am simply going to assume of the many obligations I discuss that they can have no other origin, and the reader must judge for himself whether descriptions and arguments rooted in that assumption are at all helpful' (Walzer, 1970, p. x). Pateman is another who is sympathetic to this view (Pateman, 1985). Yet, it is clear that in most cases some voluntary act or commitment is neither a necessary nor a sufficient condition for the acquisition of obligations. (It should be remembered that the term 'obligations' is being used to cover both obligations and duties.) It cannot be a necessary condition because it is unable to explain its own foundations. Any voluntarist account of obligations must rest on the prior acceptance of the proposition that people have an obligation to act in accordance with their voluntarily incurred obligations; this obligation itself cannot be based on any voluntarily acquired obligation, or else that obligation too would have to be voluntarily acquired, and we would be faced by an infinite regress of voluntary obligations. Nor is the obligation to act in accordance with one's voluntarily incurred obligations unique in this respect, for there are many commonly recognised obligations which do not have their origin in any voluntary undertaking on the part of the person obligated. These include obligations to parents and siblings, and our obligation to aid those suffering serious harm who could be easily helped at negligible cost to oneself (minimal altruism). It is very unclear how we could possibly envisage some of these obligations as arising from voluntary acts such as promises, contracts or consent. Nor, even were this possible, is it obviously morally attractive to try to so reorganise social life that they would issue from the genuinely voluntary, obligation-creating acts of each individual.

Further, as most voluntarist theorists have accepted, it does not appear that such voluntary undertakings are a sufficient condition of a person's acquiring an obligation. This is because there are some actions which a person does not have the right to do, hence could not have an obligation to do, even if that person promises, contracts or consents to do them. Consent cannot normally create an obligation to do that which is seriously morally wrong. One is not obligated to commit a murder even if one has voluntarily consented to undertake it; such commitments have no moral force. This is perhaps of some relevance to voluntarist theories which focus too narrowly or exclusively on a supposed obligation-creating act. For example, an oath of allegiance requiring one unconditionally to obey the government, no matter how voluntarily entered into, cannot reasonably be thought to issue in an obligation to obey the government whatever in fact it does. This is not to deny that one may sometimes have an obligation to obey a law which is unjust, but only to say that some actions are so unjust that nothing, and certainly not consent, could place one under an obligation to perform them. The circumstances in which voluntary undertakings can give rise to a moral obligation are always limited by other moral considerations. Consent or other voluntary commitments, cannot straightforwardly transform a vice into a virtue. Voluntarist theories of political obligation, as is widely recognised by their proponents, will always need to be part of a more complex moral picture which charts the contours within which it is possible for voluntary acts to create obligations. For this reason, voluntarist theories need to be supplemented or supported by elements drawn from at least one or other of the approaches discussed in the next two chapters.

A voluntarist theory of political obligation, therefore, does not entail, nor need it derive from, a general voluntarist account of all obligations, so neither of the above points should be read as intended to refute the more sophisticated versions of such theories. However, these reflections may help to loosen the hold that those theories have on us. This seems particularly true of the idea that consent is a necessary condition of political obligation, for if we come to see that something is not necessarily so this may be a decisive step towards seeing that it is not so at all. Thus, if some alleged voluntary obligation-creating act is neither necessary nor sufficient for the ascription of many obligations, this may make us more open to the idea that such an act is neither necessary nor sufficient for the ascription of a distinctively political obligation. It may prevent us from becoming fixated on what is only one among several possible models of obligation. Granted the difficulties within voluntarist theories outlined earlier, it may even incline us to look more closely at some of our other, non-voluntarily incurred, obligations for a better understanding of political obligation. Indeed, this is a suggestion which will be taken up and explored more fully in Chapter 6.

The second aspect of voluntarist accounts to be considered concerns their more or less explicit model of the polity as a voluntary association. Characteristically, on this view, the polity, or at least the legitimate polity, is conceived as an association constituted and sustained by the voluntary choices of those individuals who compose it. Though no doubt much more complex, a polity is not viewed as *essentially* different from those many other voluntary associations we may choose to join or leave, more or less as we please. As one defender of this understanding of a polity writes:

> 'A body politic, on this view, is a group of persons related by a system of agreements; to be a member of a body politic is to be a party to the system of agreements. The model is obviously the voluntary group or organization. A voluntary group is composed of a number of individuals who, in pursuit of a common purpose, agree to act in concert, putting themselves under a common discipline, authority and obligation' (Tussman, 1960, p. 7).

Though far from conclusive, one immediate reflection on this claim is that it does not seem to conform to the understanding many people have of their relationship to their polity, as Tussman is himself aware. People do not characteristically see themselves as having much choice in the matter of the polity of which they are members. Furthermore, if the arguments of the earlier part of this chapter are correct then this discrepancy is easily explained. The reason is that people do *not* voluntarily join their polity, usually citizenship is imposed upon them, and it is, therefore, unsurprising that people should be aware of this fact. As Neil MacCormick forcefully observes:

> 'Human societies are not voluntary associations. At least so far as concerns national societies and states, most human beings do not have a choice which one they will belong to, nor what shall be the law and the constitution of that to which they do belong; especially their belonging to a given state is not conditional upon their assenting to the basic structure of its organization' (MacCormick, 1982, p. 84).

So far as existing political communities are concerned, therefore, to conceive them as voluntary associations is fundamentally to misrepresent their character.

However, this observation has no force against those theorists who hold that only if the polity were a voluntary association would its members have genuine political obligations. What, if anything, can be said about this view? Certainly we need to ask what polities would have to be like if they were to be voluntary associations (see

Johnson, 1976). For example, what would be the position of those
who did not wish to join? Would they be permitted to reside in the
territory of a polity they did not wish to join? What would their
relation be to those who were members? What would they be
allowed to possess? On what terms could members 'resign' from
the polity? What should be done about those who wished to become
members, but whom others, already members of the polity, did not
want to allow to join? As we saw earlier, when discussing Beran's
work, some voluntarist theorists have attempted to answer some of
these questions, and they might reply, therefore, that while these,
and other similar questions which could be asked, do raise genuinely
difficult practical problems, it is still possible that with sufficient
ingenuity they could be satisfactorily resolved. It might be denied,
therefore, that such problems are in any sense fundamental objections to the voluntary association model of the polity. How
adequate is this reply?

There are at least three points which can be made in response.
First, it is surely not the case that scepticism about the feasibility of
transforming the polity into a genuine voluntary association is
simply a manifestation of complacent attachment to the status
quo. It really is extremely difficult to see how these questions could
be satisfactorily answered given even remotely plausible assumptions about human beings and the world in which we live. In part
this difficulty is a consequence of the sheer size, scale and complexity of modern advanced technological societies; but it is also a
function of the more general conditions of social order, and the
problems involved in securing sufficient agreement about the terms
of political association among even a small number of socially and
culturally homogeneous people. Second, even if tolerably practicable answers could be given to these questions, it is not obvious that
they would be as morally attractive as voluntarists seem to assume.
Indeed there is some reason to believe that they would have some
very harsh implications, for while 'voluntary association is a fine
principle for those with whom others are eager to associate, it is a
disaster for those whom others instinctively avoid' (quoted in
Johnson, 1976, p. 18). Third, and perhaps most interestingly, if
the conditions of a voluntary association could be met, we might
wonder whether what resulted could be understood as a polity at all.
The differences between a voluntary association and a polity are so
fundamental that any attempt to transform the latter into the

former might be thought to undermine those very characteristics of a polity which seem to be constitutive of it.

This last claim is certainly controversial and requires more justification than it will receive here, but two particularly significant differences between voluntary associations and polities, at least as they are commonly understood, are worth observing. First, there is the role of legitimate coercion. Though voluntary associations may in some circumstances legitimately coerce or penalise their members, such a right is effectively circumscribed by the powers allowed them by the wider political authority to which they are subject. This is not true of a polity which, since it constitutes that wider coercive authority, does not have its authority defined or circumscribed by any external body, though this is not to deny that political authority is subject to moral constraints. Secondly, voluntary associations characteristically have some more or less specific and determinate, substantive purpose which their members share. This is much less true of polities though the contrast should not be overdrawn. It is not a distinction between complete unanimity and complete absence of agreement about ends, but there does seem to be a qualitative rather than merely quantitative distinction. Disagreement about substantive political purposes seems fundamental to and ineradicable from polities and in a manner which is not so with respect to voluntary associations – a point to which we shall have occasion to return later. Taken together then, these considerations do raise serious doubts as to whether the attempt to understand or reconstruct the polity as a voluntary association is practicable, desirable or even conceivable. Such considerations are not conclusive, but nor are they negligible.

The final feature of voluntarist theories of political obligation to be considered is the understanding of the person which they generally presume. What follows on this issue is especially sketchy and tentative. There has been extensive discussion of personal identity in recent Anglo-American philosophy. Much of this work has focused quite narrowly on the problem of how bodily or psychological continuity relates to a person's persistence over time, though some of this has been interestingly connected to wider moral and social issues (Parfit, 1984; Williams, 1973). However, issues of selfhood have also recently assumed an increasingly important role in some areas of political theory, stemming particularly from the work of Charles Taylor (Taylor, 1989) and Michael Sandel (Sandel,

1982). The question which is most to the point in this context concerns what makes a person who he or she is: the question 'Who am I?' Characteristically voluntarist theories assume, for the matter is rarely discussed in detail, a view of the person which may seem at first glance admirably commonsensical, robust, non-metaphysical and unproblematic. Persons are conceived as separately existing entities, only contingently related to each other and to their social context, possessed of natural freedom and some minimal measure of reason. However, this picture and, in particular, the portrait of persons as possessing natural freedom, in opposition to the constraints imposed by social life, is potentially misleading. It is not so much that the necessity of some social context for a person's development is not appreciated, but that the connection between the person and that social context is seen as essentially contingent rather than entering into the person.

Voluntarist theorists, at least in recent times, have been suspicious of attempts to connect a conception of the person in some deeper way with the social context in which persons are formed. Typically, they have preferred to ask 'What sort of life shall I choose to lead? and to resist the question 'Who am I?' This latter question is viewed as both metaphysically confused and politically dangerous; often being seen as damagingly associated with the obscurity of Teutonic idealist philosophy and the political fanaticism of totalitarianism and extreme nationalism. Moreover such suspicions are not without justification. However, even where this 'atomic' conception of the person does not ignore the general point that a person is in part a product of society – and the pervasive attraction of the idea of a state of nature to voluntarist theorists is in some cases evidence of a reluctance to accept even this – there is a marked failure to appreciate the more specific point, that *particular* persons are in part the products of *particular* societies. There is an obvious sense in which if we had been born and raised in a different society we would be different people; not only because we would be a different genetic bundle, but because our formative experiences would be different. Of course the specific formative experiences of each of us are different but there is also a significant discontinuity between different polities. One of our important formative experiences is the development of our sense of being a member of this particular political community. Personal identity, our sense of who we are, is partly constituted by where we are born, resident and educated; and it is partly a function of the history, culture and rules of our community which confer a particular status on us and from which we necessarily acquire some self-understanding. In part our identity is bound up with the polity of which we are members, and it would not be surprising if this connection between the sense of who we are and the polity of which we are members were reflected in our conception of political obligation.

Much of the substance of these reflections on personal identity could be conceded, at least for the sake of argument, yet it might still reasonably be asked what specifically they show about political obligation. There seem to be at least two questions which need to be answered. First, how closely are the socially constituted elements of the person tied to distinctions between polities? There is, it has been suggested above, some connection but it is not clear how deep or extensive this must be. Second, even if some deep connection is established between the identity of persons and the polity of which they are members, what are the precise implications of this for their political obligations? These are difficult questions but they will be left until Chapter 6 since, as with the discussions of the nature of obligation and the voluntary association model of the polity, these reflections on personal identity are largely intended to prepare the ground for the account of political obligation that is advanced there. They attempt to do so in two ways. First, through undermining the plausibility and appeal of the manner in which these issues are usually treated within voluntarist theories. Second, through intimating the kind of treatment which might prove more satisfactory, they suggest that what is required is an account of political obligation in which the obligation is not created by a person's voluntary undertakings; a conception of the polity which is not modelled on a voluntary association; and an understanding of the person more deeply rooted in membership of the polity.

This chapter has been concerned with only one type of justification of political obligation, though one of great resilience in the history of political philosophy. It has tried to show that voluntarist theories do not give us a plausible understanding of political obligation. More ambitiously, it has been further argued that the terms in which such theories conceptualise the problem may effectively preclude its resolution. In arguing this, however, I would not wish to be understood as denying either that voluntarism plays an important role with respect to some features of our moral life, or the significance of such matters as civil rights and democratic freedoms to which some, though not all, voluntarist theories give such prominence. A political community in which people have the rights associated with citizenship within liberal democracies is, for example, in my view, preferable to one in which they are lacking. My concern, however, has been to deny that these features succeed in furnishing the conditions of a convincing voluntarist theory of political obligation. The next chapter, therefore, addresses a different approach to justifying political obligation – an approach in which voluntarism plays no significant part.

3 Teleological Theories

In the preceding chapter we considered and largely rejected one broad category of accounts of political obligation. In this chapter a very different type of account will be the subject of attention. Whereas voluntarist theories seek to justify political obligation in terms of some putative voluntary undertaking by the person obligated – a specific utterance or sequence of actions – which puts the person under the obligation, the theories discussed in this chapter approach political obligation from a different perspective. These theories seek to explain political obligation by looking to the future rather than to past actions, and by looking to the likely consequences or the purposes of the obligation, rather than to some obligation-creating voluntary commitment. These theories are classified as teleological because they explain political obligation in terms of some goal, end or purpose, a *telos*, which provides the moral ground or justification of this obligation. Political obligation within teleological theories characteristically derives from a general requirement to act in a manner which will bring about the best possible state of affairs. Teleological theories, therefore, are typically consequentialist or purposive in structure: an action, practice or institution is to be judged solely in terms of the value of what it achieves. Where teleological theories divide sharply one from another is in their accounts of the nature and value of these purposes or consequences. Thus while all teleological theories account for political obligation by reference to the beneficial purposes or consequences of the obligation, and the obligation is derivative from these purposes or consequences, they often disagree both about what these are and about what makes them valuable.

It was suggested in the previous chapter that voluntarist theories of political obligation essentially conceive political relations as the result of individual choices or commitments, and polities as voluntary associations. In contrast teleological theories model polities rather differently: typically the polity is conceived as a means to achieve valuable ends. Correspondingly the relationship between the individual and the polity is basically instrumental, though according to some teleological theories membership of a polity may be partly constitutive of the good to be achieved. While it would be a mistake to overdraw this contrast, since the reasons for joining a polity on a voluntarist view are also likely to be instrumental, it remains the case that the two types of theory are significantly different in their approach to political obligation. Within voluntarist theories it is the voluntary undertaking, the act of consent or allegiance, which is fundamental to grounding political obligation; within teleological theories there is no need for any voluntary undertaking, for what grounds political obligation are the ends which it serves, and these do not depend upon some voluntary act on the part of the person obligated. Political relations are not explained or justified by their being the subject of a voluntary agreement, but by their being instrumental to the achievement of valuable ends. Thus a polity is not a voluntary association, or more accurately need not be, and even if it were the obligation deriving from it would derive not from its being voluntary, but from its being instrumental to the achievement of valuable ends. In short, therefore, while voluntariness is not strictly incompatible with a teleological account of the polity it is neither a necessary nor a sufficient condition of political obligation. On a teleological interpretation, political obligation is independent of the voluntary undertakings of those obligated.

This detachment of political obligation from the voluntary undertakings of the person obligated has the obvious result that teleological theories will avoid the besetting problem of voluntarist theories. Voluntarist theories, whatever other difficulties they face, seem unable to overcome the problem of discovering or characterising a plausible voluntary undertaking which is the basis of political obligation. Since teleological theories do not depend for their validity upon some such undertaking they will not confront this difficulty. In this respect at least teleological theories have a clear advantage over voluntarist theories. Most teleological theories also possess a second advantage: such theories are usually part of a comprehensive and more or less unified moral theory. Many teleological theories, including the most popular and fully developed of such theories, utilitarianism, purport to provide complete moral theories in a way that voluntarism characteristically cannot. It is often unclear precisely how voluntarist principles of political obligation fit within a wider moral context and how they relate to other moral principles. For reasons mentioned in the previous chapter voluntarism cannot provide a self-sufficient moral theory; at the very least it seems to depend upon some prior non-voluntarist commitment of the form that a promise or consent obligates. Many teleological theories, however, are either single-principle theories, such as utilitarianism, or clearly prioritise different principles and hence furnish a comprehensive and unified moral theory. This is not, though, a necessary feature of such theories since it is possible to specify ends which are both plural and either conflicting or incommensurable. Where there is no hierarchy of values or where values are incommensurable, then the place of political obligation may be much more complex and difficult to elucidate with any precision within the overall moral theory.

Two types of teleological theory will receive particular attention in this chapter. There is no suggestion that these exhaust all possibilities and each in turn admits of a variety of interpretations, but they are much the most widely canvassed of teleological theories. These are the utilitarian and common good accounts of political obligation and each will be discussed in turn. Rather more attention will be devoted to utilitarianism, not because it furnishes a more interesting or more plausible account of political obligation, but rather because it is a very widely held and much elaborated moral theory, especially within the philosophical community at the present time. Common good accounts on the other hand have been less fashionable, especially of late, and have also received less theoretical development. Both theories, it will be argued here, fail to provide convincing general accounts of political obligation, though utilitarianism will be found to have less to offer than the common good approach. However, it should be noted, especially in the case of utilitarianism, that the failure to provide a cogent account of political obligation need not be viewed as a failure for utilitarianism as a moral theory, nor typically will it be by utilitarians themselves. It can be argued that a satisfactory account of political obligation is not essential to the adequacy of a moral theory; but as my concern is with political obligation rather than with the wider question of the adequacy of utilitarianism as a complete and comprehensive moral theory, it is only utilitarian accounts of political obligation which will be considered. In fact utilitarianism has been subject to extensive theoretical criticism but much of that, while important, will not be addressed in what follows (e.g. Williams, 1985, esp. Ch. 6). Only criticisms specifically relevant to political obligation will be introduced here, though inevitably one's view of this issue is likely to be closely connected to one's overall evaluation of the merits of utilitarianism.

The structure and forms of utilitarianism

Utilitarianism is a moral theory which, in its simplest and most straightforward form, judges the rightness of acts, practices and institutions exclusively by their tendency to promote utility, or happiness. Utilitarianism is probably the most fully elaborated and discussed of all moral theories within contemporary philosophy. This process of refinement has led to the development of significantly different strands within a broadly utilitarian approach. However, there is some unity in the diversity, for as R. G. Frey has written:

> 'the term "utilitarianism" refers not to a single theory but to a cluster of theories which are variations on a theme. This theme involves four components:
> (1) a consequence component, according to which rightness is tied in some way to the production of good consequences;
> (2) a value component, according to which the goodness or badness of consequences is to be evaluated by means of some standard of intrinsic goodness;
> (3) a range component, according to which it is, say, acts' consequences as affecting everyone and not merely the agent that are relevant to determining rightness;
> (4) a principle of utility, according to which one should seek to maximize that which the standard of goodness identifies as intrinsically good' (Frey in Miller, 1987, p. 531).

Utilitarianism therefore judges actions in terms of their producing a particular kind of consequence for a specific group of beings.

However, utilitarians often disagree among themselves about how these elements are to be specified. For example, the nature of the value of the consequences to be promoted has been variously characterised as pleasure, happiness, desire-satisfaction, well-being, welfare and utility. Clearly these are not all equivalent to each other. There have also been disagreements about the scope of the theory: does it apply to all sentient creatures (including animals) or only to human beings? Does it apply across generations and does it apply to potential people? The way in which these questions are answered will have important implications, for example, for what ecological and environmental policies should be pursued. Furthermore, utilitarians also disagree about the appropriate form that maximisation should take. Should the aim be to maximise the sum total of utility (however conceived) or instead, average levels of utility? Which of these principles is adopted is likely to have radically divergent implications for population policy: the former, aggregate utility, will incline towards a large number of people with relatively low levels of utility, while the latter, average utility, will favour a smaller number of people with in general higher levels of utility. These are merely some examples of a range of questions to which utilitarians have given different answers. It is impossible here either to survey all these variations or to attempt to evaluate the several differing strands within utilitarianism; some simplification, therefore, is not merely desirable but unavoidable. In what follows, two axes of disagreement which are especially significant will be considered: that between act- and rule-utilitarianism and that between direct and indirect utilitarianism. However, as a preliminary, a few very brief remarks about the development of utilitarianism may be appropriate.

Historically utilitarianism emerged as a fully self-conscious moral theory with the work of Jeremy Bentham but substantial elements of the theory significantly predate his work. The search for origins is not an especially fruitful activity and either Godwin or Paley might have claim to the primacy I have attributed to Bentham, but there is one predecessor of Bentham who particularly merits brief mention. David Hume, in the mid-eighteenth century, developed a broadly utilitarian account of political obligation as an alternative to the social contract theory of which he was a most trenchant critic. Among the more important of his criticisms of social contract theories was his recognition that the basis of the obligation to keep the contract cannot itself be contractual. For Hume the obligation that we have to keep our promises, of which the social contract is only one example, in turn rests upon an obligation to promote the general interest (and ultimately upon self-interest). Hence, Hume argued that reference to a social contract is redundant, because we can base our obligation to government directly on our obligation to promote the general interest, without recourse to an, in any case largely fictional, social contract (Hume, 1953; 1978, Bk III, Pt II, Sects VII and VIII). For Hume political arrangements were devices, historically evolved, to protect people against the exigencies of the human condition and aimed at securing the benefits of a stable political order. Hume's utilitarianism, however, was blended with a conservatism which inclined him to view existing institutions, merely by virtue of their evolution and convenience, as utilitarianly justified.

In this respect Bentham, a radical reformer, endlessly engaged in designing new and better institutions, was of a very different cast of mind. However, rather surprisingly perhaps, despite his antipathy to Hume's conservatism, Bentham has very little of interest to say about political obligation. Bentham's enthusiasm for ridiculing contract theory was no less than Hume's, but he did not add much of substance to those criticisms and his positive account of political obligation is disappointingly thin. It consists of not much more than observing of the duty of subjects to their government that: 'they should obey in short so long *as the probable mischiefs of obedience are less than the probable mischiefs of resistance* . . . taking the whole body together it is their *duty* to obey, just so long as it is in their *interest* and no longer' (Bentham, 1988, p. 56). Of course political theorists are not required to be equally interested in the many questions which they could address, but in his comparative neglect of political obligation Bentham seems to have been something of an example to later utilitarians who, for the most part, have had little to say specifically about this issue. However, this neglect is more than a matter of lack of interest. One reason why Bentham, and other radical utilitarians, have had little to say about political obligation is precisely because they have wanted to deny that there is any general political obligation. They are not, therefore, even attempting to justify political obligation but consciously seeking to undermine it. This is not, though, the only reason why utilitarianism has had so little of interest to say about political obligation.

A further reason relates to the structure of the simplest and most straightforward form of utilitarianism; though whether or not Bentham was an exemplar of this form of utilitarianism is a matter of vigorous scholarly debate (see e.g. Kelly, 1990, esp. Ch. 3). Act-utilitarianism judges an action to be morally correct if it maximises beneficial consequences, however such consequences are precisely defined. On this view, how a person ought to act in a given set of circumstances should be exclusively determined through a calculation of the likely general utility of the various courses of action available. That act should be chosen which will have, to the best available knowledge, the largest net balance of beneficial consequences over harmful ones. Act-utilitarianism requires the consequences of each act to be weighed and the decision how to act to be based on a calculation specific to the particular choices and circumstances facing the agent. Such an approach, however, will have obvious difficulty in generating a general theory of political obligation; at best it seems likely that it may issue in some rules of thumb or rough maxims of conduct (for example, obeying the law will usually be more generally beneficial than breaking it). The bottom line of act-utilitarianism is that articulated by Bentham: citizens should obey government when it is for the best, but not obey when disobedience is for the best, and there is little more to be said. Of course this is what act-utilitarianism will recommend about any practice or institution, and obedience to the government will be no different. However, whatever its other merits, this form of utilitarianism is singularly ill-fitted to provide an account of general obligations deriving from special relations, including a distinctively political obligation. This is an important problem which will be pursued further in the next section.

The requirement of act-utilitarianism that each and every act be evaluated on its utilitarian merits, however, has seemed to some utilitarians to be too simple, and to ignore both the uncertainty and the costs involved in making such judgements about each and every action. While perhaps reasonable with respect to small-scale decisions, act-utilitarianism seems more problematic when applied to complex decisions, involving a wide range of possible actions, a complicated computation of probable consequences, and where an individual's knowledge is likely to be very imperfect. The difficulty of some of these calculations, their costliness in terms of time, energy and other resources, the propensity of peoples' calculations to give undue weight to their own interests rather than the social benefit, and above all the uncertainty induced in others who have to rely on such, possibly faulty, calculations has led some to adopt a more sophisticated form of utilitarianism known as rule-utilitarianism. According to rule-utilitarianism it is better in many circumstances that people do not rely on their own uncertain calculations in deciding what to do but instead should follow a general rule.

Rule-utilitarianism dictates that people should be guided in how to act by a general rule about the best way to act in circumstances which fall under the rule. The rules should be devised in the light of generalisations about what action, or which kinds of action, in these sorts of circumstances, are most likely to maximise the beneficial consequences. For example, according to rule-utilitarians, most utility will obtain not if each person asks him or herself whether or not the killing of another person in any particular instance may be maximally beneficial, but by requiring everyone to observe laws prohibiting murder whatever the circumstances. Thus the kind of calculation undertaken by Raskolnikov in Dostoyevsky's novel, *Crime and Punishment*, which apparently justified his murdering a rich but cruel and mean money-lender for the greater social good, would be precluded. Rather we should all follow a rule prohibiting murder to avoid such disastrous miscalculations. Rule-utilitarianism, therefore, seems a potentially more promising approach to political obligation because it is better able to accommodate the institutional dimension of political obligation. For political obligation has to do with the relationship between individuals and their polity, and whereas act-utilitarianism is tied to assessments of specific actions, rule-utilitarianism appears able to give a more adequate account of practices or institutions, which are at least partially constituted by complex structures of rule-governed relationships.

One immediate difficulty about rule-utilitarianism, however, is whether it is a genuinely coherent alternative version of utilitarianism or whether it is essentially unstable and, on closer inspection, collapses back into act-utilitarianism. This is not an issue which can be pursued in any depth here but the nature of the problem at least must be stated (see Lyons, 1965). Rule-utilitarianism appears to confront a dilemma: either it must approve the violation of a rule in circumstances where such a violation will clearly be more beneficial than observing the rule; in which case it appears to be merely a more sophisticated form of act-utilitarianism, and rules are not obligatory but simply helpful guides to action. Alternatively rule-utilitarianism does hold that the rules are obligatory even when violating them would be more beneficial; in which case it does offer a genuine alternative to act-utilitarianism, but one which seems from the perspective of maximising utility to be irrationally concerned with following rules for their own sake. In short, either rule-utilitarianism collapses into act-utilitarianism or it engages in a kind of 'rule-worship' which is utilitarianly unjustified. The problem here is that if the violation of a rule will be more beneficial, particularly if it is clearly more beneficial, then observing it in such circumstances seems irrational, given utilitarianism's overriding concern to maximise beneficial consequences. The most plausible response to this problem has been to stress the beneficial consequences of the rules, the stability and predictability they provide, which any sanctioned violation of the rules will inevitably undermine. The difficulty with this defence is that while it has some plausibility in marginal or uncertain cases, in others where the violation of a rule is obviously beneficial it seems justified only by placing an infinite weight on the beneficial effects of observing the rules. Such a strategy then seems to be motivated only by a desire to validate rule-utilitarianism and not by any empirical observation of the likely consequences of rule violations. In that respect such a strategy is entirely inconsistent with the spirit of utilitarianism.

Before proceeding to consider further the relationship between these types of utilitarianism and political obligation there is another distinction which it is useful to introduce – the distinction between direct and indirect utilitarianism. This distinction does not straightforwardly map on to that between act- and rule-utilitarianism though it is closely related to it. The distinction between direct and indirect utilitarianism is more concerned with questions of motivation than of outcome. In its simplest form it would appear that utilitarianism requires that actions be motivated by a desire to maximise utility (in some form or other). However, it was recognised fairly early in the development of utilitarianism, Sidgwick being among the clearest exponents of the view, that it may not be true that utility will be maximised if people directly and consciously aim at maximising it (Sidgwick, 1874). It may be more productive of utility, at least in some circumstances, if people act on a motive other than that of maximising utility: in such circumstances utility will be maximised indirectly, as a consequence of pursuing some other aim. Thus indirect utilitarianism severs any tight connection between the good (maximising utility) and any particular motivational assumptions. In this respect it is easy to see how indirect utilitarianism is related to rule-utilitarianism but it is also important to see that indirect utilitarianism is a more encompassing category than rule-utilitarianism. Indirect utilitarianism implies nothing specific about the way in which utility will be maximised, other than that it is not always attained through the direct attempt to achieve it: it may or may not be best achieved by following rules in the manner recommended by rule-utilitarianism. Thus rule-utilitarianism may be understood as one form of indirect utilitarianism but it is not the only one.

On first encounter, indirect utilitarianism may appear a peculiar doctrine. It might seem that if the best situation is one in which utility is maximized then *a fortiori* it would be most likely to be achieved if people aimed at its attainment. However, this inference is fallacious as can be seen if one thinks, for example, of personal happiness. It is far from self-evident, and indeed there is a considerable body of experience to contradict the claim, that personal happiness is maximised through its direct pursuit. It seems that happiness is often best achieved indirectly, as a by-product of the pursuit of other aims and with other motivations. Similarly, social utility may in fact be maximised through means other than its direct pursuit. For example, there might be some moral analogy to the invisible hand of the free market which, according to classical economic theory, produces the economically most prosperous society from people's self-interested pursuit of their own economic advantage. This shows how the general good might be maximised as an unintended consequence of very different intentions and motivations. (The truth or otherwise of classical economic theory is beside the point for the purposes of this illustration.) Indirect utilitarianism, therefore, claims only that the best state of affairs might not result from people directly aiming to achieve the best state of affairs.

Utilitarianism and political obligation

This detour into some of the intricacies of utilitarianism is important because these refinements provide the most promising materials for a response to perhaps the most powerful objection to any utilitarian theory of political obligation. This objection, which was briefly mentioned in the previous section, has been stated most clearly and forcefully by A. J. Simmons (Simmons, 1979, pp. 45–54). He argues that there is a structural feature of act-utilitarianism which precludes its providing a satisfactory theory of political obligation. Act-utilitarianism, as we have seen, requires us to act in whatever way will in fact maximise utility and this requirement is entirely general. There is, therefore, within this perspective no place for such particularised bonds as political obligation – the special relationship between individuals and their own polity. Thus, in discussing Bentham's account of the citizen's obligation to obey the law Simmons writes:

> 'Bentham's approach to problems of political obedience fails in obvious ways to yield an account of political obligation. Act-utilitarian calculations, as Bentham suggests, may lead us to conclude that we ought to obey but they may lead us as well to conclude that we ought to disobey on some other occasion (or perhaps support the political institutions of some other countries). Insofar as the conditions influencing the results of these calculations are by no means constant, we can derive from the simple act-utilitarian approach no moral requirement to support and comply with the political institutions of one's country of residence. There will be no particularized bonds on this model; at best, it seems obligations will be to comply when doing so is optimific' (Simmons, 1979, p. 48).

Simmons argues, therefore, that act-utilitarianism is structurally ill-equipped to provide an account of the kinds of obligation implied by a theory of political obligation. At best it can develop a rough rule of thumb that, by and large, it is right to support and comply with the institutions of one's country. However, act-utilitarianism has nothing specific to say about the nature of that relationship nor why there is, or should be, any special relationship between members and their polity. Of course, as stated earlier, this need not be an embarrassment to act-utilitarians; from their perspective any account of political obligation may be unnecessary or mistaken. However, if we are looking for an account of the kind of obligations of which political obligation is an example, act-utilitarianism is unsuited to the task.

Simmons' claim that act-utilitarianism is, by virtue of its structure, incapable of providing a theory of political obligation, is similar to our earlier conclusion, and is, in my view, convincing. However, his treatment of rule-utilitarianism is less satisfactory, and about indirect utilitarianism he is almost silent. Simmons' rejection of rule-utilitarianism depends entirely upon the argument that if it is to remain consistently utilitarian it will necessarily collapse into act-utilitarianism. As he puts it, 'while the rule-utilitarian's principles of obligation will have the kind of force we want in providing an account of political obligation, these principles will not be capable of a utilitarian defense' (Simmons, 1979, p. 52). He offers no other arguments against a rule-utilitarian account of political obligation. He also fails sufficiently to distinguish 'rule' from 'indirect' utilitarianism: it is far from self-evident that the standard objections to rule-utilitarianism apply to all indirect utilitarianisms, or at least if they do this needs to be argued rather than assumed. Thus it is both desirable and necessary to say a little more about the relationship between utilitarianism and political obligation. It is desirable in the case of rule-utilitarianism since, though the arguments against it as an independent form of utilitarianism may be convincing, it would strengthen the case against a rule-utilitarian account of political obligation if there were other arguments against it. It is necessary in the case of indirect utilitarianism since it is less evident that all forms of indirect utilitarianism must collapse into act-utilitarianism.

One feature common to all forms of utilitarianism is that they are 'maximising' moral theories. Utilitarianism requires us to maximise the beneficial consequences of actions and practices. This is important because even rule and indirect utilitarianism would have to show that political obligation involves practices which do not merely have beneficial consequences but which *maximise* those beneficial consequences. In short, whatever is understood by political obligation, if it is to be utilitarianly justified, must be shown to be maximally beneficial. One noteworthy point is that it is very rare for utilitarians of any sort after Hume to attempt to demonstrate the validity of this claim. Bentham, as we have seen, made no such attempt, nor have many of his successors. Usually such attempts as have been made, for example that by R. M. Hare, point to the very considerable benefits that are supposed to flow from having a system of law and a stable political order. However, it seems implausible to think that these benefits will always outweigh the benefits of other options, or that such benefits are necessarily threatened by substantial levels of non-compliance with the law. Nor, to repeat another point, is it at all clear to what extent these arguments establish particular obligations between persons and *their* polity. Thus, for example, the kind of disutilities associated with disobedience to the law usually apply quite generally: they do not relate specifically to disobeying the law of the particular political community of which a person is a member. The utilitarian argument will be that obedience to the law, in whatever polity, is likely to have considerable utility. But this is not enough to provide an account of political obligation.

Indirect utilitarians could argue that utility is best promoted by a world in which individuals recognise a special obligation to the polities of which they are members. While many of the particular acts which may be enjoined will not directly maximise utility, so it could be argued, overall utility is still best maximised indirectly through people meeting their political obligations to their own polity. This is not a line of thought which is addressed by critics such as Simmons, but equally it does not appear to be a line of thought much favoured by utilitarians. While an account of political obligation in these terms would meet the requirements of a theory of political obligation, it is surely short of persuasiveness from a utilitarian perspective. First, the claim that overall utility will be promoted in such a manner appears to be an act of faith rather than based on a clear-headed calculation of consequences. Second, it would be obviously implausible for utilitarians to present political obligation as a blank cheque. The requirements of political obligation would need to be 'cashed out' but doing so might leave little scope for a general political obligation. What would be the point of such an obligation, even within an indirect utilitarian theory? It may have some useful motivational role as political rhetoric, but as is often the case with indirect utilitarianism, it can function in this role only by requiring people to believe what from the perspective of utilitarianism itself is untrue: that is it might be utilitarianly best if we all believed there was a general political obligation, even though this belief is false. Other than as a defence of indirect utilitarianism such dubious moral casuistry has little to commend it (Williams, 1985, pp. 106–10).

Hare's utilitarian account of political obligation

Some of the considerations we have been discussing can be brought together by examining in a little more detail the arguments of one of the most sophisticated of utilitarians. R. M. Hare is one of the few contemporary utilitarians who has specifically addressed the problem of political obligation. For Hare political obligations are 'the *moral* obligations that lie upon us because we are citizens of a state with laws' (Hare, 1976, p. 2). He concentrates particularly on the obligation to obey the law though he recognises that this is not the only such obligation. He also acknowledges 'that this obligation may lie, not only on citizens, but also on anybody, even an alien, within the jurisdiction (most people think that foreign visitors too have a moral obligation not to steal)' (Hare, 1976, p. 1). It is important, however, to note the significance of this acknowledgement. First, and most fundamentally, it seems to transform the question that Hare originally asked. What started as a question about our obligations as citizens of a particular state becomes a question about whether there is a quite general obligation to obey the law. If even an alien has this obligation, then it is not specifically an obligation of citizenship, though of course it may be an obligation citizens share with others. Second, a further source of confusion is introduced by his example of stealing. It is likely that most people will think that there is a moral obligation not to steal, whether or not there is a legal prohibition on stealing. Hence even the revised question of whether there is an obligation to obey the law may be muddled by choosing an action which is likely to be thought wrong independently of whether there is a law prohibiting it (though in fairness to Hare nothing in his argument depends upon this possible confusion).

Hare then briefly explains his own form of utilitarianism and how he has been led to it. He writes:

'To ask what obligations I have as a citizen is to ask for a universal prescription applicable to all people who are citizens of a country in circumstances just like those in which I find myself. That is to say, I have to ask – as in *any* case when faced with a question about what I morally ought to do – "What universal principle of action can I accept for cases just like this, disregarding the fact that I occupy the place in the system that I do (i.e. giving no preferential weight to my own interests just because they are mine)?" This will lead me to give equal weight to the equal interests of every individual affected by my actions, and thus to accept the principle which will in all most promote those interests. Thus I am led to a form of utilitarianism' (Hare, 1976, p. 3).

He recognises that we could ask the question he identifies above directly in each and every case, but if we did no general principles would be required. However, for Hare there are reasons why we need general principles:

> 'In practice it is not only useful but necessary to have some simple, general and more or less unbreakable principles, both for the purposes of moral education and self-education (i.e. character formation) and to keep us from special pleadings and other errors when in situations of ignorance or stress. Even when we have such principles we *could* disregard them in an individual case and reason it out *ab initio*; but it is nearly always dangerous to do so, as well as impracticable; impracticable because we are unlikely to have either the time or the information, and dangerous, because we shall almost inevitably cheat, and cook up the case until we can reach a conclusion palatable to ourselves. The general principle that we ought to obey the law is a strong candidate for inclusion in such a list as I shall be trying to show; there may be occasions for breaking it, but the principle is one which in general there is good reason for inculcating in ourselves and others' (Hare, 1976, p. 4).

Hence Hare articulates briefly and lucidly the standard arguments for some form of indirect utilitarianism, and suggests how he will show that the general principle, that we ought to obey the law, can be utilitarianly justified. There are, however, several observations to be made about the argument contained in these extended quotations, though the wider issue about whether utilitarianism does indeed follow, as Hare claims, will not be addressed. This last point, while very important to any overall assessment of Hare's utilitarianism, is tangential to our concern with political obligation, and in any case it could not be discussed without considering much more fully his detailed arguments for these conclusions (Hare, 1963, 1981).

The first point again concerns his equivocation about whether the duty to obey the law is an obligation specifically connected with citizenship or membership of a particular polity, or whether it is an entirely general moral requirement. Second, and connectedly, much will depend upon how 'circumstances just like these' are to be identified and characterised. To what extent, for example, do they

permit variations between polities? This is important in determining
the scope of the obligations. Do they apply only to people living in
'liberal democratic' states much like the Britain in which Hare is
resident? Do they apply to anyone living in any polity? Would they
apply equally, or at all, to illiberal, undemocratic, or even totalitar-
ian states? Third, it is unclear what the precise status is of the
general principle that we ought to obey the law. Hare concedes that
there may be occasions when the law should be broken, but how are
such occasions to be identified unless some judgement is made about
the situations in which the law should not be obeyed? It is natural to
assume that such judgements will be made according to utilitarian
criteria. The status of the principle would then appear to be more
that of a rule of thumb, a guide to conduct or a summary of
experience but no more. Yet Hare believes such general principles
are not mere rules of thumb and that, for reasons largely to do with
moral education and the dangers of partiality, we ought to inculcate
sentiments which will encourage people to feel badly about violating
such general principles, even though, on his own account, such
people may have acted rightly.

For Hare political obligations are those 'which arise only because
there is a state with laws' (Hare, 1976, p. 5), and in discussing a
hypothetical example he identifies three reasons for obeying the law
which provide specifically political obligations. His hypothetical
example concerns hygiene laws requiring delousing to prevent the
spread of typhus. There are several good moral and prudential
reasons why one should do what the hygiene laws require, as Hare
observes, but there are three moral reasons specifically related to the
existence of the law. These are:

'1.   The fact that, because there is an enforced law, resulting in
      general delousing, failure to delouse myself will harm
      people's interests much more, by making them *very much*
      more likely to get lice or typhus;
2.   The fact that, if I break this law, it will cause trouble to the
      police in catching me, thus rendering necessary the employ-
      ment of more policemen, who therefore cannot grow yams
      instead, and so harming the interests of the people who could
      have eaten the yams;
3.   The fact that if I break this law, it may encourage people to
      break this or other laws, thereby rendering a little more likely

(a) the removal of benefits to society which come from the existence of those particular laws, and (b) the breakdown of the rule of law altogether, which would do great harm to the interests of nearly everybody' (Hare, 1976, p. 7).

He further remarks that the second and third reasons 'are subsidiary, but have the important property that (except for 3a) they might survive even if the law in question were a bad or unnecessary one whose existence did not promote the general interest' (Hare, 1976, p. 7). Again there are several comments which it is appropriate to make concerning Hare's argument.

At the risk of repetition, the first point is that none of these reasons applies specially to people as citizens rather than to anybody who happens to be geographically proximate. In fact the first reason applies more to geographically proximate persons whether or not they are citizens, than it does, for example, to relatively isolated citizens having less physical contact with other people. The first reason also has two other distinctive features. Most crimes are not contagious in the manner of typhus, hence it is a very special and unusual feature of this example that the cost of not observing the law is likely to be literally contagious (by contrast with what might be called the metaphorical contagiousness suggested by the third reason). The first reason also depends upon the law's being effective, not merely in the sense that it is generally observed, but in the further sense that it will actually prevent the spread of typhus. If the law required something which did not in fact decrease the likelihood of the spread of typhus, then the first reason would not provide a good justification for obeying it. This is important because it shows that the merits of the first reason are largely independent of there being a law, but depend instead upon two other considerations: that the 'advice' contained in the law is good advice and that most people follow it. This can be seen, for example, in the case of exhortations to take precautions to stop the spread of AIDS. There is no legal requirement to engage only in 'safe' sex, yet if the advice is good and most people follow it then Hare's first reason applies equally to this case, entirely independently of whether or not there is a law compelling such safeguards.

The first reason, therefore, seems to have little if anything to do with specifically political obligation, and the weight of the argument for political obligation must be borne by the other reasons, which Hare himself regards as 'subsidiary'. The second reason does have some force but it is surely weak: while it is a general reason for obeying all laws it is also a reason against laws generally. The enforcement of a law always has costs and if this were the principal reason for obeying a law then it would be better to repeal it. These costs of disobeying a law are entirely dependent upon the existence of that law and could be eliminated by abolishing the law. Furthermore, if policemen are a necessary deterrent to law break-ing, which is likely to be part of their utilitarian justification, then it is doubtful whether a single violation of a law does impose any significant extra costs (but see Parfit, 1984, Sects 28, 29). The first part of the third reason, like the first reason, depends upon the particular law having beneficial effects. Further, when the costs to me of observing the law amount to more than the benefits to others of my observing it, then it seems that the law ought to be broken. Evidently the second part of the third reason is intended to block this kind of calculation, or at least significantly to tilt the balance in favour of law-abidingness, yet it seems that even quite high levels of law breaking do not lead to the breakdown of law altogether. The net effect of one instance of law breaking will usually be negligible in the context of the preservation and maintenance of a system of law and order.

The force of these utilitarian reasons becomes weaker still when this last objection is further elaborated. It can be argued that it is quite reasonable and seems to be utilitarianly justified to act on the principle that breaking a law is morally right, when more utility will be derived from violating the law and so long as it is known that the conduct of others will not be affected by this violation. In this case, as in many others, the objection of the utilitarian is not to violating the law, but to being found out. Hare does consider this complaint and claims that such a view is unsatisfactory because it ignores people's desire not to be taken advantage of. He, therefore, suggests adding a fourth reason for obeying the laws to those listed earlier:

'The fact that, if I break the law, I shall be taking advantage of those who keep it out of law-abidingness although they would like to do what it forbids, and thus harming them by frustrating their desire not to be taken advantage of' (Hare, 1976, p. 11).

Unfortunately while this may be a good reason for obeying the law it is not a reason which is obviously available to the utilitarian. Richard Dagger has argued that the plausibility of Hare's contention must depend upon the plausibility of the assimilation of the frustration of any desire to a harm; yet, he argues, such an assimilation is unconvincing (Dagger, 1982). For example, if in a fair race my opponent continually beats me, then he frustrates my desire to win but still he has not harmed me. Dagger's claim has considerable force so far as our ordinary use of the term 'harm' is concerned; however, it is not inconsistent for a utilitarian to claim that the frustration of any desire is a harm to the person whose desire is frustrated (though possibly a very small one, and perhaps often outweighed by other harms).

The problem which faces Hare is the less obvious one of how the desire not to be taken advantage of is to be interpreted. The position of people who obey the law is *ex hypothesi* not worsened by those who break it, so how are they harmed? It seems that the desire not to be taken advantage of is really an independent moral principle – basically a requirement of fairness – masquerading as a desire. It is notoriously the case that utilitarianism, with its intrinsic indifference to distributive questions, has considerable difficulties in accommodating such requirements. At the very least if it is permissible to posit the desire not to be taken advantage of, then it is presumably also legitimate to represent many other non-utilitarian moral commitments as desires; a move which leads to such enormous complications that most utilitarians have sought to avoid it. On the other hand, where systematic attempts have been made to incorporate a range of diverse values within utilitarianism, one begins to doubt whether there is very much left of the theory which is distinctively utilitarian (e.g. Griffin, 1986).

These reflections show how Hare's attempt to articulate a utilitarian theory of political obligation is fraught with serious difficulties. The most fundamental of these is the persistent tendency, clearly exhibited in Hare's argument, to transform questions about political obligation into more general questions about right conduct which quite simply fail to address the issue of the specific obligations of citizens to their own polity. This is not strictly a logical implication of rule- or indirect-utilitarianism, but it is a tendency to which utilitarians of all hues seem naturally inclined. Taken together with the criticisms made earlier (and of course a whole range of objections to utilitarianism as a moral theory more generally which have not been considered here), they suggest that the prospects for a convincing utilitarian theory of political obligation are at best unpromising. Those few theorists who have sought to incorporate a substantial utilitarian component within their justifications of political obligation have invariably done so in a highly qualified manner (Flathman, 1972); and there have been few if any attempts to articulate a fully elaborated theory of political obligation in uncompromisingly utilitarian terms. Since utilitarianism is a far from underdeveloped theory this is of itself a most significant indication of its limitations in this area.

Political obligation and the common good

The second kind of teleological accounts of political obligation to be considered in this chapter are best known as 'common good' theories. The core of this approach is to argue that political obligation derives from the common good; and the common good may be either that of a particular community or of everybody. This common good, on either interpretation, provides the basis of the obligations of members to their polity. By contrast with utilitarianism, the common good is usually understood as a qualitative conception, including within it moral qualities which are regarded as intrinsically valuable, and does not consist of the mere maximization of desire–satisfaction, pleasure or happiness. Unfortunately terminological confusion abounds in the area, for not only is the common good on occasion used to mean utility-maximisation, but the term 'public interest' which is sometimes used as a synonym for general utility, may also be used to mean a non-utilitarian conception of the common good (e.g. Milne, 1990). However, the key point is that the common good, as we shall use it, is a more or less specific qualitative conception of the good life, which is distinct from, and often antithetic to, the maximisation of utility.

Political obligation on this view depends entirely upon whether the political arrangements of a community promote the common good. This theory, which in some forms has an affinity with Rousseau's conception of the general will, perhaps receives its fullest exposition in the work of the nineteenth century English idealist philosopher, T. H. Green. Interestingly he also appears to have been the first political philosopher explicitly to use the term 'political obligation', by which he meant 'the obligation of the subject towards the sovereign, of the citizen towards the state, and the obligations of individuals to each other as enforced by a political superior' (Green, 1986, Sect. 1). Green's theory is rich and complex and has deserved better than the rather cursory and dismissive treatment it has mostly received in modern discussions of political obligation (e.g. Simmons, 1979; Green, 1988). It offers a more fruitful approach to political obligation than that of the much more fashionable consent theories – the account of political obligation to be defended in Chapter 6 certainly owes something to it – and it is encouraging to see it receiving more sympathetic treatment among some recent commentators (e.g. Harris, 1986, 1990; Milne, 1986; Nicholson, 1990). However, common good theories of political obligation are not without difficulties of their own, some of which will be considered in evaluating Green's account.

As with utilitarianism, though having a very different content, Green's account of political obligation is part of a comprehensive moral and political theory. Inevitably this larger context can only be briefly touched upon here. One way of viewing Green's moral and political theory is as an attempt to rescue and reconcile the valid insights of both individualism and collectivism. Green believed that the end of the moral life is self-realisation – in this respect there are some close affinities with J. S. Mill's views on self-development – but he also believed that an essential means to self-realisation was the framework afforded by life within a state. Self-realisation for Green can only be achieved through willing the common good; a good which is common to everyone. Anything which is necessary to the achievement of the common good is necessarily good for everyone. The state, therefore, should be understood as 'an institution for the promotion of a common good' (Green, 1986, Sect. 124). Green rejects any conceptualisation of the problem of political obligation in which the individual and the state are seen as inherently antagonistic, but he is also clear that collectivities have no value apart from their contribution to the self-realisation of individual human beings.

Green's view of the relationship between individual self-realisation and social and political institutions is well encapsulated by

Harris and Morrow in the Introduction to their edition of his *Lectures on the Principles of Political Obligation*. They write:

> 'Green argues that the essential social dimension to individual self-realisation means that the individual must regard social institutions and practices (political organisations, customs, mores, law) as collective efforts after a common good. They are the result of the need to secure and maintain the conditions within which individuals can pursue their self-realisation in their own ways, and of the need to harmonise the ways in which they do so. As such, these institutions and practices need to be acknowledged by the individual as deserving his allegiance and consideration as essential to his own self-realisation – provided they continue to act as means to the common good and not as impediments to it' (Green, 1986, pp. 6–7).

Political obligation for Green, therefore, depends entirely upon the polity promoting the end of self-realisation. It is important here to be as clear as possible about the precise relationship between self-realisation and the political community: individual self-realisation is impossible outside of a polity, and the polity is an essential means to self-realisation – but not just any polity promotes self-realisation. Political arrangements have to be of the appropriate sort if they are to facilitate self-realisation: political obligation is owed only if the political arrangements are of a kind which will further individual self-realisation. Hence the so far basically formal accounts of self-realisation and the common good have to be provided with a substantive content, and most of Green's moral and political philosophy is concerned with elucidating and justifying a particular interpretation of self-realisation and the common good.

For Green, institutions, including political institutions, can promote self-realisation only indirectly, by developing and protecting the conditions within which it becomes a feasible object of endeavour. Self-realisation can be achieved only through free action, and neither the state nor any other institution can guarantee its attainment, much less act as a surrogate on behalf of the individual. What the state should secure are the circumstances within which individuals can act to realise themselves. Thus the state must have a form which facilitates everyone's attempt at self-realisation. The state does this through the maintenance of a structure of rights, a structure which protects everyone's ability to pursue their own self-realisation and mediates and harmonises the varying aspirations of its citizens. Such rights, therefore, are not merely the creation of the state in the sense that rights are whatever the state says they are: Green is not a legal positivist about rights, though these moral rights should be incorporated within a legal structure, if they are to be effective. Yet neither are these rights natural – they have no place in some putative state of nature – for self-realisation cannot be achieved apart from social relations and life within a polity. As Green expresses the matter:

'It is on the relation to a society – to other men recognizing a common good – that the individual's rights depend . . . A right is a power claimed and recognized as contributory to a common good. A right against society, in distinction from a right to be treated as a member of society, is a contradiction in terms . . . If the common interest requires it, no right can be alleged against it' (Green, 1986, Sect. 99).

Rights moreover are in a continuing process of historical development, adjusting to people's increasing recognition of the conditions under which self-realisation is possible. Rights for Green therefore are neither natural nor simply a child of law, and their basis lies in a morality of self-realisation rather than in some pre-social nature or the sovereign power of the state.

Where then does this leave Green's account of political obligation? In brief, political obligation is owed to a state by virtue of its supporting and maintaining a structure of rights, which is both an essential element in the common good and a necessary means to any individual's self-realisation. Such an obligation is dependent upon the state's actually contributing to this end: the sovereign power of the state exists to maintain a structure of rights which contributes to the common good. As Green makes explicit:

'If the power, existing for this end, is used on the whole otherwise than in conformity either with a formal constitution or with customs which virtually serve the purpose of a constitution, it is no longer an institution for the maintenance of rights and ceases to be the agent of a state. We only count Russia a state by a sort of courtesy on the supposition that the power of the Czar, though subject to no constitutional control, is so far exercised in accordance with a recognized tradition of what the public good requires as to be on the whole a sustainer of rights' (Green, 1986, Sect. 132).

The state is a moral entity which derives its character from its effectively incorporating the essential conditions of the common good. Political obligation is parasitic upon a state's being a genuine state in Green's understanding of what this requires. Political obligation derives from the instrumental but essential role of the state in achieving the common good; facilitating for each and every individual the active pursuit of their own self-realisation.

Green's moral and political theory has been subjected to comprehensive criticism by commentators such as Pritchard (Pritchard, 1968, Ch. 4) and his account of political obligation has been criticised in a similar vein by Plamenatz (Plamenatz, 1968, Ch. 3). It is not possible here to assess the merits of all these criticisms, though it is worth noting that Green's work has also recently attracted some careful and thoughtful defenders (e.g. Nicholson, 1990). However, the element of Green's political philosophy which is most crucial to his theory of political obligation is his account of the common good, and this is the focus of attention in the following discussion. Its main contention will be that his account of the common good is fundamentally flawed and in a way which crucially damages his theory of political obligation. However, the judgement of Green's most virulent critics will not be endorsed: there are some important positive lessons to be learned from Green's approach.

The most prevalent and potentially destructive criticism of the idea of the common good is that it is either impossible to determine or non-existent. How are we to decide what is in the common good? How are disputes to be adjudicated? Is there a good which is common? One, perhaps obvious, source of these questions lies in the fact of disagreement: there is widespread disagreement between people about what is good both for themselves and more generally. At some very general level it might be widely agreed that people cannot achieve their good apart from being members of a particular political community, yet of itself this does not imply any agreement about the shape or form of that polity. Similarly, for example, both socialists and libertarians might agree with Green that the state should maintain and protect individual rights, yet there would be little overlap in their accounts of the nature and content of these rights. Of course Green offers his own account of these rights but one does not need to be a radical sceptic to be less than optimistic about any such account carrying widespread conviction. Arguments about basic political values, and especially arguments about rights, are very rarely compelling. Indeed, one of the most important reasons why political authority is necessary is precisely because people have different conceptions of the (common) good, and these differences are frequently incapable of resolution through rational argument. In such circumstances it is hard to see what appealing to the common good can be expected to achieve. It is true that if the common good is left sufficiently vague or abstract then agreement is more likely, but this will merely disguise substantive disagreement about which policies will in fact further the common good. While the common good may appear to be a unifying conception, at least within the conditions of modern societies, this appearance is largely illusory.

This last point hints at a more radical criticism of Green's use of the common good, which is that it is conceptually confused. Goods can be common in the sense that different people hold the same things to be valuable but they are not common in the sense that one person's good is the same as that of another. For example, most people value health and in this sense health is a 'shared good' but it is not a common good. There is no sense in which your health and my health are common; there is no common good 'health' in which we both share. It is only in a metaphorical sense that we can be said to 'share' good health. Yet it seems that Green's argument requires him to employ the concept of the common good in this illicit sense, for he argues that in promoting the common good each person is promoting something which is also in his or her own individual good. There are, it must be conceded, some distinctive goods, so-called 'public goods', which do possess a feature which makes such a claim much more plausible: this feature is their indivisibility. A standard example of such a good is clean air: clean air is a good which, subject to certain qualifications, can be enjoyed by everybody or nobody. Thus in helping to keep the air clean I can be said to be promoting the common good because one and the same good – the clean air – is simultaneously good for both myself and others. For the most part, though, these do not seem to be the kind of goods Green has in mind. However, since his conception of self-realisation, of which the common good is an essential component, is also a thoroughly moralised conception, one might ask whether this moralised conception avoids these difficulties.

The answer must be that it does not, because Green fails to recognise the possibility of genuine conflict between an individual's personal interest or good and the common good. For Green the common good is also necessarily in each and every individual's personal interest, and to think differently is to misunderstand one's true interest. It would be wrong to deny that such misunderstandings occur – people can be short-sighted and mistaken about their own interests: but when insisted upon as a necessary truth – that any apparent conflict between personal interest and the common good must be illusory – the claim becomes a metaphysical one, with some potentially sinister implications. It is, for example, a line of thought similar to that which led Rousseau to conclude that people can be 'forced to be free' (Rousseau, 1973, p. 177). While Green did not intend these more sinister implications, the inadequacy of his argument remains. The point is well expressed by A. J. Milne, one of Green's most sympathetic critics:

> 'He [Green] ignores the fact that a man's personal self-interest can conflict with the interest of his community . . . According to him, what is morally right is always in a man's personal self-interest because they are the same. Failure to see this betrays an unenlightened conception of personal self-interest. But they are the same only because Green has made them so by definition. This is unacceptable because it obscures the real sacrifice of personal self-interest, which meeting moral demands may involve; for instance, risking one's life on military service' (Milne, 1986, p. 69).

This denial of the possibility of conflict between the common good on the one hand, and both competing moral obligations and personal self-interest on the other, is a fundamental failing within Green's account of political obligation. It also marks a clear difference between his theory and the account of political obligation to be defended later: that also attaches deep significance to membership of a political community and what this implies, but it denies that political obligation can always be integrated or harmonised with other moral obligations or our personal self-interest.

Nor, indeed, should it be assumed that where such conflict arises primacy must always be granted to political obligation.

It seems that Green's account of political obligation is, therefore, dependent upon an account of the common good which is deeply flawed. Inevitably this must seriously impair his account of political obligation. However, as I have indicated, though Green's employment of the common good is unsatisfactory, he is right to see an important connection between political obligation and the shared conditions of life which constitute membership of a polity. This is a line of thought which will be developed in Chapter 6. Green's own account of political obligation, though, is too inextricably bound up with difficulties surrounding his conception of the common good and the idea of self-realisation to be rescued in its present form. However, while Green's tendency to conflate within the common good all potentially conflicting values is a consequence of a desire shared with many common good theorists – to construct a coherent, integrated and harmonious moral system – this is not a necessary feature of such theories. It is possible to advance a common good theory which admits the possibility of serious conflicts of interest and moral conflict. All such theories, though, must address the problem remarked earlier, of identifying and characterising the common good; a problem which is especially daunting with respect to complex, plural and ethically diverse societies such as most modern states.

It is ultimately the combination of a commitment to some more or less substantive conception of a common good and their teleological structure which accounts for the limitations of common good theories of political obligation. Common good theorists are right to stress the importance of membership of a particular political community to any adequate account of political obligation, but it is their interpretation of this relationship which is misguided. In part it is the understanding of a polity as an instrument for achieving a shared substantive good which is at the root of this problem. This is not necessarily to deny that there are any common goods, nor that people's relationship to their polity is not in some respects instrumental, but it is to suggest that membership of a polity cannot be adequately comprehended within these terms. It may be helpful to introduce a comparison to illustrate this point. Most people recognise obligations to other members of their family, but it would be a misrepresentation of these obligations to think of them primarily in terms of promoting the common good of the family. While such obligations usually imply a special concern for the well-being of other members of our family, our actions are only rarely informed by any conception of the common good of our family. Of course such an idea is not meaningless, but in this respect a family is, for example, unlike a voluntary association committed to the pursuit of a common substantive purpose. While there are many important disanalogies between a family and a polity, in this respect our membership of our political community is more like our membership of a family. than our membership of any association (voluntary or otherwise) primarily devoted to the pursuit of a shared substantive purpose and identified by reference to some supposed common good.

It must be emphasised that this point about the relationship between membership of a political community and a conception of the common good is a subtle one. The distinction between different kinds of relationship or association which I have sketched is a matter of degree: it would also be foolish to deny that there is wide variation between polities, and within one polity at different times. It is, it ought to be acknowledged, also a distinction which owes much to that drawn by Michael Oakeshott between what he calls 'civil association' and 'enterprise association' (Oakeshott, 1975, II). However, I have deliberately chosen not to articulate the distinction in Oakeshott's terms, partly because in my view he is sometimes prone to exaggerate it; and partly because his account of it is at times closely bound up with his own valuations of different political arrangements. The particular point which needs to be stressed in the context of common good theories of political obligation is that even when the members of a polity are united in the pursuit of one overriding common good – as is sometimes the case during wars when the survival of the polity itself is at stake – that common good is not what characterises membership of the political community. The polity cannot be *identified* with, for example, the winning of the war; for the polity preceded the war and, if successful, will survive it. Political obligation transcends any attempt substantively to characterise a common good.

This chapter has examined teleological theories of political obligation in general and two specific forms in particular. Both the common good and utilitarian theories were found deficient as general accounts of political obligation. It is not my claim, however, that they have been refuted. The arguments of political philosophy are seldom conclusive, but weighty considerations have been advanced to show that, especially in the case of utilitarianism, they do not offer very convincing general theories of political obligation. Inevitably this chapter has not attempted a complete or comprehensive discussion of teleological theories, but enough has been said to reveal their most important inadequacies and limitations. The next chapter considers an approach to political obligation which is neither teleological nor voluntarist. This will then complete our survey of the principal theories of political obligation.

4 Deontological Theories

It has been argued in the preceding chapters that both voluntarist and teleological theories have considerable difficulty in providing convincing accounts of political obligation. Voluntarist theories, though superficially attractive, present a picture of political relations which largely misrepresents people's actual experience of political life: teleological theories are either unable to tie political obligation to a particular polity or resort to unconvincing conceptions of the common good. Voluntarist and teleological theories both fail to capture distinctive features of political obligation. However, there is one further type of account which attempts to avoid the failings of the other two theories. This type of account seeks to explain political obligation in terms of the idea of duty and therefore may be called 'deontological'.

It is perhaps doubtful whether what will be grouped together here as deontological theories really do constitute a rigorously distinct type of theory of political obligation. In different forms they seem to have connections with both voluntarist and teleological theories. In particular, for example, the entire class of voluntarist accounts could be interpreted as a species of deontological theory; that is, in terms of a duty to keep our voluntary undertakings. Indeed, one of the objections to voluntarist theories was precisely that they require some such moral underpinning since they are unable to account for the bindingness of voluntary commitments in their own terms. What this kind of problem reveals is the dangers of attaching excessive significance to any classification of moral and political theories, including that employed in this book. The basis of most classifications is pragmatic rather than metaphysical; they help to illuminate the logical structure of different theories. I would, therefore, defend the usefulness of the tripartite categorisation employed here, even though in some respects it must be conceded that the borderline between deontological and one or other of the alternative types of theory is difficult to draw with any precision. In the case of deontological theories in particular, however, it is necessary to treat this classification with some flexibility.

The central idea informing deontological theories is that political obligation must be justified in terms of an account of our duties which are explained neither as the result of our voluntary undertakings, nor simply in terms of the promotion of some good or valuable end. The basic distinction between teleological and deontological ethical theories is lucidly presented by Richard Norman:

'A teleological theory is one which asserts that an action is right or wrong, in so far as it produces good or bad consequences . . . A deontological theory is one which asserts that at least some actions are right or wrong, and we have a duty or obligation to perform them or refrain from them, quite apart from considerations of consequences. Teleological theories thus treat "good" and "bad" as the basic ethical concepts, and define others such as "right" or "wrong" in terms of these, whereas deontological theories would treat "right", "wrong", "duty" and "obligation" as basic, or at least give them equal status with "good" and "bad"' (Norman, 1983, p. 132).

According to deontological theories the moral rightness or wrongness of some actions is independent of whether or not they maximise utility, promote the common good or contribute to the achievement of any other end. Rather, these actions should be judged morally by whether or not they are required or prohibited by some general moral principle(s) or system of duties. In their most extreme form, often associated with Kant, they deny any moral significance to consequences, but in a more moderate form they claim only that there are some actions which we are either required to perform, or required to refrain from performing, whatever the net balance of beneficial or harmful consequences. A typical example of such an action for many deontologists is our duty not to lie. On this view telling a lie is often wrong, even if doing so would promote happiness, minimise suffering or have other beneficial consequences. Deontological theories of political obligation, therefore, justify it in terms of a general moral principle or some system of duties. In what follows two deontological theories in particular will be considered: first, the fair-play theory and second the theory of a natural duty to uphold just institutions. However, we shall begin with a discussion of the idea of 'hypothetical consent'; an approach which apparently closely links deontological theories with voluntarist accounts of political obligation.

Hypothetical consent

The crux of hypothetical consent is that it is *hypothetical*: that is, it does not involve showing that consent is in fact given; only that it would or should be given. Hypothetical consent, therefore, needs to be supported by arguments which establish that such consent is rationally or morally required in the appropriate circumstances. As has been argued earlier, in Chapter 2, 'hypothetical consent' cannot properly be understood as a genuinely voluntarist theory of political obligation. However, it may be useful to sketch briefly how it can be seen, nevertheless, to emerge from that tradition of thinking. A fundamental problem for voluntarist theories, it will be recalled, is that of identifying some action or undertaking on the part of citizens which could reasonably be identified as a voluntary act giving rise to their political obligations. Tacit consent was one response to this difficulty, but, as has been shown, it does little to solve the fundamental problem. A further worry about voluntarist theories is their susceptibility to the objection that people sometimes consent to arrangements which are irrational, unreasonable or unfair. While in some circumstances it may be thought proper to hold people to such arrangements on the basis of their consent, in others their consent is inclined to be overridden or nullified by the irrational or morally unacceptable nature of the arrangements. Within voluntarist theories this last point is usually taken account of by characterising the circumstances of voluntary agreement in such a way that indisputably irrational, unreasonable or unfair agreements will not meet the conditions for voluntary consent. However, this attempt to circumscribe the conditions under which consent should be understood as genuine can be taken in one of two directions. The first is that favoured by voluntarist theories, which is to look for specific actions which meet the appropriately described conditions, but this search, it has been argued earlier, has not met with much success. The second is to dispense with actual acts of consent altogether, and instead focus upon what it would be rational, reasonable and fair to agree to under the appropriately described circumstances. These considerations would then have force regardless of whether or not people in fact consented.

From this perspective actual consent drops from the picture. The important question becomes not whether people do or did actually consent to some particular government or political system, but what it would be fair, reasonable and rational for people to agree to within appropriately characterised circumstances. It is this move which marks the transition from actual consent theories (explicit or tacit) to hypothetical consent theories – 'hypothetical' because there is no actual consent, only 'hypothesised' consent; a consent hypothesised on the basis of what would be fair, reasonable and rational in the relevant circumstances. The question for hypothetical consent theorists is not whether a person does consent but whether he or she ought to consent. Indeed it is important to appreciate just how far 'hypothetical consent' departs from actual consent, for it is not merely that actual consent is not a necessary condition of hypothetical consent, it need not be a sufficient condition either. Actual consent is at best a piece of evidence about what it might be reasonable or rational to consent to: within the theory of hypothetical consent it is redundant. Hence the earlier argument to the effect that the logic of hypothetical consent is categorically distinct from that of voluntarist theories.

A further feature of this transition which should be noticed is the enhanced role of the *theorist* of political obligation. Within voluntarist theories, there is an irreducible role for agents in the real world: it is *they* who do or do not consent. Though within voluntarist theories there is a recurrent tendency to circumscribe such contingencies, they cannot be eliminated entirely if such theories are to retain their genuinely voluntary basis. It is of course this element of voluntariness which is the prime attraction of such theories. However, within hypothetical consent theories there is no role for agents in the real world. Their 'choices' are modelled and determined by the political philosopher or theorist; it is the theorist's arguments which establish the validity of 'consent' and not the actions of agents in the real world. Hence there is no need to look to the histories and actions of actual people, instead it is the theoretical arguments of the philosopher which are crucial.

Perhaps the clearest account of hypothetical consent is provided by Hanna Pitkin (Pitkin, 1972). She develops her account in the process of interpreting the arguments of Locke and Tussman; but our interest is not in the adequacy of these interpretations but in her account of hypothetical consent. According to her, what is important is not whether consent is actually given but the basis upon which one ought to consent. The fundamental issue then becomes one about the grounds upon which such consent is morally required. In short, there is a decisive shift within hypothetical consent theory away from the actions of the people consenting to the qualities and attributes of the government or political system which would justify consent. According to Pitkin the relationship between consent and obligation in hypothetical consent theory is the reverse of that within voluntarist theories:

> 'It is not so much your consent . . . that obligates you. You do not consent to be obligated, but rather are obligated to consent . . . you are obligated neither by your own consent nor by that of the majority but by the consent rational men in a "hypothetical state of nature" would have to give' (Pitkin, 1972, p. 61).

Thus it is the reasons for 'consent' and not the fact of consent which explain political obligation. The argument shifts entirely to what it would be rational or obligatory to consent to in appropriately specified circumstances. Thus

> 'your obligation to obey depends not on any special relationship (consent) between you and your government, but on the nature of the government itself . . . In one sense this "nature of government" theory is thus a substitute for the doctrine of consent. But it may also be regarded as a new interpretation of consent theory, what we may call the doctrine of *hypothetical* consent. For a legitimate government, a true authority, one whose subjects are obligated to obey it, emerges as being one to which they *ought to consent*, quite apart from whether they have done so. Legitimate government acts within the limits of authority rational men would, abstractly and hypothetically, have to give a government they are founding. Legitimate government is government which *deserves* consent' (Pitkin, 1972, pp. 61–2).

While it is unfortunate that Pitkin should persist with the idea that 'hypothetical consent' might be regarded as a 'reinterpretation' of consent theory, confusion between the logic of voluntarist theories and 'hypothetical consent' is deeply enshrined within the social contract tradition.

What Pitkin demonstrates is that 'hypothetical consent' offers a very different kind of theory from voluntarist accounts of political obligation. Indeed, it now begins to look as if it may be hard to distinguish hypothetical consent from some kind of teleological theory. What is clear, however, is that 'consent' seems to have ceased to do any useful or distinctive work in the theory and it has become largely honorific in status: its role almost seems to be to provide us with reassurance that our obligation really results from our voluntary choice even when it does not. This recourse to what is essentially a comforting subterfuge is no doubt a tribute to the tenacity of voluntarism in much of our thinking in this area. However, granted that hypothetical consent is not a form of voluntarism, how persuasive an approach is it to the problem of political obligation?

The status of hypothetical agreements or choices is an issue which has been frequently discussed in recent political philosophy. Much of this discussion has been generated by the arguments of John Rawls' *A Theory of Justice*, though he does not present a 'hypothetical consent' account of political obligation (Rawls, 1971). His account of political obligation, at least in that book, is in terms of a natural duty to support just institutions and will be considered later in this chapter. However, as is well known, the idea of a hypothetical contract is central to his account of how we are to arrive at principles of justice. For Rawls, principles of justice are those that would be agreed upon by rational and reasonable people in circumstances that are accepted as fair. This requires us to think ourselves into what Rawls calls 'the original position'; a situation in which we are shorn of the kind of knowledge which would enable us to bias principles of justice in favour of our own interests or our own conceptions of the good. The original position is characterised by its being a fair situation in which to decide on principles of justice. However, as Rawls makes clear, this is a thought-experiment and there is no literal sense in which a social contract results. One criticism to which this line of argument has given rise, which applies equally to hypothetical consent theories of political obligation, concerns how people can be morally obliged by an agreement or contract that they have not in fact entered into. As Ronald Dworkin has trenchantly remarked: 'a hypothetical contract is not simply a pale form of an actual contract; it is no contract at all' (Dworkin, 1975, p. 18). Or as Jean Hampton puts it, 'If someone tells me a story in which hypothetical people make hypothetical contracts, how does that story have any effect on what I am *bound* to do?' (Hampton, 1986, p. 268).

Such objections are decisive against 'hypothetical consent' where genuine consent is claimed to be the basis of the obligation. However, they have little force if it is recognised, as it is by Pitkin (and Rawls), that actual consent is essentially irrelevant to the argument. Certainly it is mysterious how consent which was not given, or an agreement which was not entered into, can *of itself* be morally binding. (What it might be asked does 'of itself' refer to here since *ex hypothesi* there was no consent or agreement?) This is an issue which needs to be explored more fully. It is true that, in some circumstances, to show that we would have agreed to something even though in fact we did not, may provide us with a good reason for acting *as if* we had agreed. For example, if reasonable efforts were made to seek my agreement to some course of action, but for non-culpable reasons I could not be contacted, and if the action was undertaken in good faith, then I may accept that the fact that I would have agreed does bind me to support that course of action. I may reasonably accept this even though if I were asked now I would not agree. For example, suppose I am in business and my partners enter into an arrangement correctly believing that I would have agreed to it. They therefore expect me to bear my share of the costs and are prepared to give me my share of the anticipated rewards. However, by the time I am asked I can see that the arrangement is not going to result in the anticipated rewards, and, therefore, it would be to my advantage not to be a party to the arrangement. Nevertheless, the fact that I would have agreed could reasonably be thought to bind me to my share in the arrangement: I would be treating my partners unfairly by exploiting the benefit of hindsight, if I were not to accept the arrangement to which I would have agreed.

It might appear that this kind of example will at least provide a toehold for hypothetical consent as a basis for political obligation. Unfortunately for proponents of 'hypothetical consent', however, this kind of example provides less support for their position than might at first appear. The reason is that this is a rather special kind of example, an instance of what might be called hypothetical *actual* consent. This is not, however, characteristically the kind of hypothetical consent involved in theories of political obligation. A modification of the example should make clear what is involved. Suppose now that I would not in fact have agreed to the arrangement that my business partners have entered into. I would have accepted (perhaps not explicitly in discussion with them but still in truth) that the arrangement was the best one that could have been made, but I would not have agreed to go along with it because it was suggested by a partner whom I intensely dislike: I would have preferred an apparently less beneficial arrangement which had not been proposed by that partner. How do I react now if I am told by my partners that though they accept I would not in fact have agreed nonetheless we all believe that the arrangement they entered into was at the time the most reasonable course of action? It seems far from clear in this example that I am under any obligation to be bound by their agreement. What, though, if I am told that had I been rational and reasonable I would have agreed (and I may accept that acting on the basis of disliking my partner would have been irrational and unreasonable)?

One certainly cannot be so cavalier as to say that what is reasonable and rational provides no reason for acting, but it is also true that such a reason is not based upon a person's consent. The reason is in fact a reason only if it is true that the arrangement was the rational and reasonable course of action. What this example brings out is that this reason is entirely independent of my consent or agreement; indeed it directly conflicts with the fact that I neither did nor would have agreed to the arrangement. Thus this kind of 'hypothetical consent' may conflict not merely with whether I did consent but with whether or not I would in fact have consented; that is, with my hypothetical actual consent. Again the conclusion to which this leads is that hypothetical consent has little to do with consent but is really a theory about what constitutes good reasons for action. Thus though there is a sense of 'hypothetical consent' which does genuinely connect with voluntarism and which could in some circumstances provide a reason for binding an agent on the basis of an action (the giving of consent) which is only counter-factually true; this is not the sense of hypothetical consent typically employed in hypothetical consent theories of political obligation.

There are of course good reasons why such theories do not employ the idea of hypothetical actual consent. First, as with more

straightforward versions of consent theory, it is impossible to show
that many people have in this sense hypothetically consented to
their government or political system. Secondly, while in some
circumstances hypothetical actual consent may generate obligations, there are others in which it clearly does not. The fact that I
would have placed a bet on a particular horse in a race had I not
been unavoidably detained does not entail that I am subsequently
obliged to pay the stake to the bookmaker when the horse loses (any
more than he would be obliged to pay me if the horse wins!). It is no
doubt a difficult and complicated matter to distinguish those
circumstances in which hypothetical actual consent does generate
obligations from those in which it does not. However, any theory of
political obligation employing such a notion of consent would need
to do so: it would have to show, not merely that people would have
hypothetically actually consented, but also that the appropriate
circumstances obtained for the consent to warrant the attribution
of an obligation. In short, unsurprisingly, hypothetical actual
consent faces similar difficulties to those confronting actual consent
theories of political obligation discussed in Chapter 2.

Thus the remaining type of hypothetical consent, perhaps best
called hypothetical rational consent, is therefore not a genuine
consent theory at all, or at least, in the terminology employed
earlier, it is not a voluntarist theory. Rather it is best understood
as a theory of good reasons, and as applied to political obligation it is
a theory of good reasons for obeying the government or respecting
the political system. Such a theory explains political obligation in
terms of our duty towards the state or government. However, having
distinguished a type of hypothetical consent theory which is distinct
from voluntarist theories, the problem now becomes how far this
theory can be distinguished from teleological accounts of political
obligation. In short, is hypothetical consent a logically-distinct kind
of duty-based account of political obligation different from teleological theories? In order to answer this question we need to focus
more directly on the nature of the duty which explains political
obligation. If the duty derives entirely from the promotion of a
particular goal, such as maximising utility, then hypothetical consent
is simply a disguised teleological theory. However, if, as is more
usual, the duty is not entirely explicable in these terms, then
hypothetical consent implies some underlying deontological theory.
Here I shall examine two attempts to provide a deontological basis

for political obligation; both of which as it happens have been advanced at different times by John Rawls. These two accounts are the 'fair-play' theory and the 'natural duty to uphold just institutions', though I shall also mention other possibilities in passing. We will begin by considering the fair-play theory.

Fair-play and political obligation

The fair-play account of political obligation appears to have been first formulated by H.L.A. Hart (though he does not use the expression 'fair-play') and subsequently developed by John Rawls. Interestingly Hart specifically relates the fair-play theory to the social contract tradition. He argues that social contract theorists were right to recognise that political obligation is 'something which arises between members of a particular political society out of their mutual relationship' but were wrong to identify this 'situation of mutual restrictions with the paradigm case of promising' (Hart, 1967, p. 63). The fair-play theory, therefore, shares with social contract theories the idea that political obligation involves an essentially reciprocal relationship, but explicitly dispenses with any residual voluntarist component of such theories. The key elements of the fair-play theory are characterised by Hart as follows:

> 'when any number of persons conduct any joint enterprise according to rules and thus restrict their liberty, those who have submitted to these restrictions when required have a right to a similar submission from those who have benefitted by their submission. The rules may provide that officials should have the authority to enforce obedience and make further rules . . . but the moral obligation to obey the rules in such circumstances is *due to* the co-operating members of the society, and they have the correlative moral right to obedience. In social situations of this sort (of which political society is the most complex example) the obligation to obey the rules is something distinct from whatever other moral reasons there may be for obedience in terms of good consequences (e.g. the prevention of suffering); the obligation is due to the co-operating members of the society as such and not because they are human beings on whom it would be wrong to inflict suffering' (Hart, 1967, pp. 61–2).

In this way Hart distinguishes the fair-play theory from consequentialist, particularly utilitarian, theories, in addition to social contract theories. The core idea informing the principle of fair-play is an underlying conception of reciprocity – that the distribution of the benefits and burdens of membership of some body or group must be fairly shared. Thus, for example, it is sometimes argued that where terms and conditions of employment are negotiated by a trade union it is reasonable to require everyone in that employment to be a member of the union. By requiring this, it is claimed, nobody benefits from the terms and conditions negotiated by the union without bearing their share of the costs. Unfortunately, Hart's own statement of the principle of fair-play is tantalisingly brief, and his concern with political obligation is subsidiary to his attempt to provide a justification for natural rights. It is better, therefore, to consider the fair-play theory through Rawls' more extended elaboration of it.

There are some differences of detail between Hart and Rawls in their exposition of the fair-play theory, but the substance of their accounts are very similar. This similarity is readily apparent from the following passage:

'Suppose there is a mutually beneficial and just scheme of social cooperation, and that the advantages it yields can only be obtained if everyone, or nearly everyone, cooperates. Suppose further that cooperation requires a certain sacrifice from each person, or at least involves a certain restriction of his liberty. Suppose finally that the benefits produced by cooperation are, up to a certain point, free: that is the scheme of cooperation is unstable in the sense that if any one person knows that all (or nearly all) of the others will continue to do their part, he will still be able to share a gain from the scheme even if he does not do his part. Under these conditions a person who has accepted the benefits of the scheme is bound by a duty of fair play to do his part and not to take advantage of the free benefits by not cooperating' (Rawls, 1964, pp. 9–10).

Rawls proceeds to develop his account in more detail but there are already at least three components of this statement of the principle of fair-play which give rise to difficulties, especially in the context of a theory of political obligation. These concern what is to count as a co-operative scheme; the requirement that the terms of co-operation be just or fair; and determining what is involved in accepting a benefit. There are other aspects of Rawls' account about which doubts might also be raised; for example, his claim that the benefits of a co-operative scheme must depend upon everyone or nearly everyone co-operating. (In fact Rawls cannot mean everyone for in such circumstances even one non co-operator would destroy the advantage, and the standard free-rider motivation for non co-operation would not apply.) Both Simmons and Greenawalt argue that the obligations of fair-play might obtain even where the acquisition of the benefit is consistent with a substantial proportion of the beneficiaries not contributing – that is, where there is a large number of free-riders (Simmons, 1979; Greenawalt, 1987). For example, one may be obliged not to walk across a lawn by a co-operative scheme requiring everyone to use the paths, even though the grass may be protected from undue wear, the object of the scheme, if only 40 per cent of people observe the requirement. This criticism of Rawls is probably correct but it is more of a technical difficulty than a serious blow to the fair-play theory. Nothing of importance would be lost if the offending condition were reformulated to avoid this criticism.

It was noted earlier in the context of Hart's statement of it, that the principle of fair-play is distinct from both voluntarist and teleological theories of political obligation. A brief elaboration of these comparisons may help to illuminate the merits of the fair-play theory, before considering the more serious objections. A.J. Simmons identifies the principal advantage of the fair-play theory as compared to consent when he writes:

'No deliberate undertaking is necessary under the principle of fair play. One can become bound without trying to and without knowing that one is performing an act that generates an obligation. Since mere acceptance of benefits within the right context generates the obligation, one who accepts benefits within the right context can become bound unknowingly. This is an important difference from consent theory's account, which stressed the necessity of a deliberate undertaking' (Simmons, 1979, pp. 116–17).

The abiding difficulty which plagues voluntarist theories of political obligation is that of plausibly explaining the voluntary undertaking by which the obligation is supposedly acquired. The fair-play account seems to circumvent this problem because its underlying model of political relations is subtly but importantly different from that informing voluntarist accounts, including consent theory. Whereas the latter basically interprets the polity as a voluntary association, the fair-play theory is premised upon a conception of the polity as an essentially co-operative structure. The justification of political obligation on this view has to do with sharing the burdens of co-operation as the price to be paid for a share of the benefits. However, the fair-play theory, while clearly dependent upon the existence of the benefits as part of its rationale, is not reducible to a teleological account of political obligation. Crucially, it is not only the benefits deriving from co-operation which justify the obligation, but also the fact that one is a participant in a co-operative arrangement which is fair. A co-operative arrangement which did not produce any benefits would be highly unlikely to justify an obligation; but, though a necessary condition of the obligation according to the fair-play theory, such benefits are not a sufficient condition. It perhaps adds to the attractions of the fair-play theory that the benefits which justify political obligation must result from a co-operative practice which is also fair.

Thus, having noted some of its merits, we should now return to the first of our areas of concern: what is meant by a scheme of social co-operation? Superficially this may seem unproblematic: a scheme of social co-operation might be characterised as working together for mutual benefit. There are, however, two issues to be raised about this apparently straightforward conception. First; it is far from clear what 'working together' or 'co-operation' requires. There are obvious examples of such co-operation: a group of people engaged in a common endeavour such as sailing a ship, playing football for the same team, making a computer together and so on. However, are two firms in a competitive market both trading legally but each trying to drive the other out of business also engaged in a scheme of social co-operation? Their respect for the law hardly seems sufficient to answer the question affirmatively for one might equally say that two states at war, if they are scrupulous in observing the various conventions and rules of war, are also engaged in a co-operative scheme. War is not mutually beneficial to the two states, but nor, presumably, is a competitive market to the two firms. Further, while both firms may agree that a competitive market provides fair terms for their conflict, does this mean they are engaged in a scheme of social co-operation?

It might be claimed that the legal structure regulating a competitive market is a means of co-operatively managing the conflict; yet while there is something to the thought that, for example, conventions governing duelling involve social co-operation, it seems odd to describe the opponents as engaged in a scheme of social co-operation. In short, there is a distinction between participating in a socially constructed practice, which may be said to involve co-operation only in a most attenuated form, and engaging collaboratively in a common endeavour for mutual benefit. While both may involve obligations it is the latter that Rawls and other proponents of the fair-play theory seem to have in mind. (It will be argued in Chapter 6, however, that political obligation would be better understood in terms of the former.) One problem for proponents of the fair-play theory of political obligation is that while there are many micro-situations within a society which provide clear examples of schemes of social co-operation in the stronger sense required by the fair-play theory, it is less clear that a society or state can plausibly be so conceived. The model of political relations as a scheme of social co-operation seems partial and incomplete: so much of politics is about coercion and the threat of coercion, about fundamental conflicts of value and interest, that it sits uneasily with what appears to be an unduly sanguine, indeed a rather cosy conception of political relations as primarily a scheme of social co-operation. Of course it would be equally one-sided to deny any place to social co-operation in an account of political life; but the overall role of social co-operation within fair-play theories shows some similarities to that of the common good within those theories, and it seems to face some similar difficulties.

One thought which has often motivated the conception of the polity as a scheme of social co-operation is some putative contrast with a state of nature. This pre-political situation is typically a situation 'red in tooth claw' or in which the life of man is 'solitary, poor, nasty, brutish and short' or at the very least lacking the 'conveniences' of society. From this perspective it is doubt about the state's being a scheme of social co-operation which is likely to appear odd. However, this gives rise to the second difficulty concerning the idea of a scheme of social co-operation. According to the fair-play theory a scheme of social co-operation must be mutually beneficial, but this implies a background or baseline against which the benefits can be measured, or at least assessed. Again the micro-examples standardly used to illustrate the theory tend to assume this background, often entirely reasonably; but what is it reasonable to assume about this background in the case of the state or society as a whole? How is this background to be characterised and justified? Is it a Hobbesian war of all against all or is it a Lockean state of intermittent transgression or even the still more benign pre-social condition described by Rousseau? Furthermore, according to at least one political theory, anarchism, the state (though not society, from which it is usually distinguished) is not a form of mutually beneficial social co-operation at all, but an instrument of exploitation and oppression. However, I shall raise doubts about the claims of anarchism in the next chapter. The point at issue here is not so much whether or not in general it is better to live within a political community – we can assume that it is – but how the distribution of the benefits of so doing is to be measured and assessed.

For the fair-play theory it is not enough that there be some baseline relative to which the polity *can* be conceived of as a scheme of mutually beneficial social co-operation, since some such baseline can always be constructed. For example, for most people a situation in which they live largely painlessly as slaves is probably preferable to one in which they suffer agonising pains for the whole of their natural lives. Yet this does not show that a system of slavery is a fair scheme of mutually beneficial social co-operation simply because we can imagine or construct some other situation by comparison with which almost everyone would find it preferable. This particular comparison is simply arbitrary and unjustified. In short, therefore, the conception of the polity as a scheme of social co-operation must be explained by reference to its being an improvement relative to some baseline or background conditions which provide an *appropriate* basis for comparison. It is this issue which is partly addressed by the claim that the terms of social co-operation should be fair or just.

It is insufficient, according to the fair-play theory, that a scheme of social co-operation be mutually beneficial: if it is to generate the appropriate obligation, it must also be fair. The reason for this requirement is that people cannot reasonably be expected to feel an obligation, even to an arrangement from which they benefit, if the distribution of the benefits and burdens of the scheme of co-operation is unfair. Suppose, for example, that two people acting co-operatively produce an extra ten units of value, and the input of each person is of equal worth (however that is measured). It will be true then that both parties benefit from this co-operative scheme even if one person receives only one extra unit and the other receives the remaining nine extra units of value. Why then should the person who only receives the one extra unit be obliged to support the scheme, even though, relative to a situation of non-co-operation, it is mutually beneficial? In short, without a requirement of justice or fairness a scheme of social co-operation can be both advantageous to all and yet exploitative (a claim, for example, Marxists would make about states with capitalist economic systems); hence the requirement that they be fair in addition to being mutually advantageous.

However, this example, through deliberate underdescription, obscures a rather large problem: that what is fair is itself highly controversial. Thus suppose we add to the example the fact that the person receiving an extra nine units also has a large number of dependants whereas the person receiving one extra unit has no dependants: how will these changed circumstances affect our judgement of the fairness of the distribution? Certainly at the level of moral intuitions there is not likely to be agreement about the answer to this kind of question; as soon as the implicit simplifying and highly unrealistic *ceteris paribus* assumptions are removed, we are confronted by a morass of diverse and conflicting judgements.

It was in large part in recognition of these conflicting ordinary moral judgements that Rawls developed his enormously influential and highly sophisticated theory of justice. The principal aim of his theory is to transcend these conflicting judgements by finding a point of view at a higher level of abstraction which would embody our agreed moral judgements, and yet also provide a generally acceptable method for adjudicating or mediating serious moral disagreement. The purpose of the construction of his original position is precisely to characterise a point of view from which we can agree on the principles which would determine a just distribution of the benefits and burdens of social co-operation. It is not feasible here to go into the details of Rawls' rich and complex theory of justice, but three general points of relevance to the fair-play account of political obligation should be noted. First, some substantial theory of justice or fairness, whether or not it is Rawls', will be necessary to fill out the fair-play account. Second, the nature of that theory will be crucial to a full explanation and characterisation of the obligation deriving from fair-play. Thirdly, neither Rawls' theory of justice nor any other has won widespread agreement, and hence even a formally shared commitment to the fair-play theory of political obligation is likely to disguise significant differences of substance as to what is implied by it. Taken together these observations, while not a conclusive argument against the fair-play theory, indicate the very real difficulties which such a theory must overcome.

The final area of concern is the claim that participants in a scheme of social co-operation 'accept the benefits' of such a scheme. Where a person voluntarily and with full knowledge of what is involved enters a scheme of social co-operation, what is meant by 'accepting' the benefits of the co-operative scheme is likely to be unproblematic. However, such clear cases cannot be straightforwardly invoked by proponents of the fair-play theory of political obligation: a crucial feature distinguishing fair-play from consent theories is that according to the former view no voluntary undertaking is necessary to acquire the obligation. It is sufficient for the fair-play theory that a person accept the benefits of a mutually beneficial and fair scheme of social co-operation. The question which arises, therefore, concerns the conditions which have to be met in 'accepting a benefit'. For example, is the mere receipt of a benefit sufficient? This seems unlikely since it gives rise to the problem of imposed benefits, first articulated by Robert Nozick (Nozick, 1974, pp. 90–3).

To explain this let us return for the moment to the simple example of a scheme of co-operation to protect the grass from excessive wear. A woman might agree that unspoiled grass is a benefit, and she might also agree that the general rule that nobody should walk across the grass involves a fair distribution of the benefits and burdens within the co-operative scheme, but does it follow that she is therefore obliged to refrain from walking across the grass if others similarly refrain from doing so? It is difficult to see how such an obligation does necessarily follow, for the woman might still prefer to walk across the grass while allowing that if everyone else acts similarly then the benefit of an unsullied lawn will be lost. It is not possible to infer from the facts that she regards the unsullied lawn as a benefit and that others are prepared not to walk across the lawn to ensure that this benefit obtains, that she must value the benefit sufficiently to oblige her not to walk across the lawn. She might simply prefer not to be inconvenienced by the detour; accept that everyone else too has the right to walk across the grass; and that if they do it is likely that the grass will be spoiled. Such a view is a reflection of her priorities: she values a nice lawn but she values her not having to make a detour more. In short, she agrees that a co-operative scheme prohibiting everyone walking across the grass would be fair and beneficial but it is not a scheme in which she wishes to participate. It is not clear, therefore, how the woman acquires an obligation to share the burdens simply because others agree not to walk across the grass and this will be sufficient to produce the benefit of an unsullied lawn.

The example of the lawn is a very simple one, and matters are obviously made still more difficult when richer and more complex political examples are considered. One need only think of problems such as the control of pollution, defence and welfare policy to see how complicated and contentious the issues are likely to become. In particular the issues become extremely thorny when the benefits from any scheme of co-operation are costly and difficult to avoid. The more a benefit is 'imposed' upon a person, and the higher the cost of producing the benefit, the more implausible looks the claim that it is simply through receiving the benefit that a person is placed under an obligation to comply with the terms of even a fair scheme of co-operation giving rise to the benefit. Thus it is reasonable to believe that 'accepting a benefit' must involve more than simply being a recipient of a benefit.

There are, principally, two lines of argument which can be advanced in response to this problem. First, stress might be laid on the idea that the beneficiaries have to be parties to, or participants in, the scheme of social co-operation and not merely beneficiaries of it: that is, what is envisaged is a genuinely co-operative structure and not the arbitrary or random imposition of benefits. The second line of thought stresses rather that the acceptance of benefits must be voluntary: acceptance is a voluntary action, hence is not something which can be imposed upon a person. Unfortunately both these strategies lead back towards voluntarist accounts of political obligation and their difficulties. The first has to confront the problem that being a member of a polity is not for the most part something over which people have much control. It might be possible to try to distinguish membership from participation, perhaps in terms of the resident/voter dichotomy, but again this seems to encounter analogous problems to those faced by consent theory. The second line of argument must address the problem that many of the benefits of living in a polity cannot realistically be rejected; hence *voluntary* acceptance seems otiose. The difficulty in this case is once more that of identifying reasonable and realistic possibilities of rejecting the benefits.

In short, therefore, the problem for proponents of the fair-play theory of political obligation is that though the idea of 'the acceptance of benefits' can be understood in either of two ways, neither has much plausibility as a justification of the supposed obligation. On the one hand, acceptance of benefits is equivalent to mere receipt of benefits; while on the other, acceptance of benefits entails a voluntary act of acceptance. The first interpretation provides a plausible account of the realities of political life – we do receive benefits about many of which we have no choice – but this does not seem to justify a corresponding obligation. The second interpretation, on the other hand, provides a potentially plausible justification of how an obligation is generated by accepting benefits, but one which has little application to the realities of political life. It is difficult to see how the fair-play theory can circumvent both of these difficulties; in consequence it seems either unconvincing or largely irrelevant as a general theory of political obligation.

Natural duty, political obligation and gratitude

The final example of a deontological theory to be considered in this chapter is Rawls' account of the natural duty to support just institutions. Before commencing this consideration, however, it should be noted that this is but one of several possible accounts of political obligation in terms of a natural duty. Kent Greenawalt, for example, distinguishes five such theories; though he does recognise that 'these theories rest on diverse foundations, and a plausible challenge to my whole enterprise is that I am treating similarly theories whose underlying bases are radically different' (Greenawalt, 1987, p. 160). Thus it is as a natural duty theory that Greenawalt considers traditional natural law arguments. This is surely unobjectionable in the sense that natural law might be taken as a paradigm example of a deontological theory, yet it also shows the awkwardness and limitations of such classifications, because the promotion of the common good tends to figure prominently in such accounts, indicating a close affinity with teleological theories. Traditional natural law theories will not be discussed here, since, in so far as they are distinct from theories which are considered, their particular features depend in some fundamental way upon a theological or deist background. Though it can be argued with some plausibility that natural law doctrine can be adapted for secular purposes, in the form of theories of human rights or various kinds of ethical naturalism for example, such an adaptation does involve their more or less radical transformation. Such secular natural law theories inevitably invoke highly contentious judgements about human nature (see Berry, 1986). In so far as traditional natural law theories are bound up with theism, however, whatever their merits, they cannot be expected to provide a general theory of political obligation which will be persuasive to non-believers; and it is obviously impossible to consider the larger questions about religious belief and the existence of God, as an aside to the main concerns of this book. For this reason, if no other, all essentially theologically based theories of political obligation will be passed over without any detailed consideration. Historically such theories have been important – the divine right of kings being one theoretically quite sophisticated example – and the resurgence of near theocratic states such as Iran suggests that in some contexts the theological justification of political obligation has continuing appeal. However, in so far as such theories employ arguments which have an appeal apart from their theological setting, these arguments are considered as part of other secular theories of political obligation.

A further reason for restricting the range of discussion of what Greenawalt classifies as natural duty theories is that the account of political obligation which will be defended in Chapter 6 shares important features with some natural duty theories, though it also needs to be distinguished from theories such as Rawls'. Greenawalt characterises a natural duty as:

> 'one that arises because one is a person or a member of a society or because one occupies some narrower status, such as being a

parent. Because such duties do not depend upon voluntary actions that bring one within their reach, their application is potentially broader than duties based on promises or fair play. In contrast with utilitarianism, theories of natural duty may explain why obedience to law is a genuine duty, not just a question of morally preferable action and why obedience may be called for though no untoward consequences will flow from disobedience' (Greenawalt, 1987, p. 159).

The aspect of natural duty accounts which, it will be argued, is of fundamental significance is the claim that political obligation has to be understood in the context of a person's membership of a polity. The account defended later will suggest a much looser connection between political obligation and obedience to the law, but it will involve a similar rejection of voluntarist, teleological and fair-play theories. However, it will also involve rejecting features of some other natural duty theories of which Rawls' version is both an interesting and influential, if not necessarily typical, example.

There will also be no sustained discussion of attempts to justify political obligation in terms of a duty of gratitude. This idea can be found lucidly and forcefully expressed as early as Socrates' claim that we owe a debt of gratitude to our political community similar to that which we owe our parents. In both cases gratitude is merited because of the succour and support which they have provided (Plato, 1969, pp. 90–1). This analogy between the duty we owe our parents and the duty which we owe the polity has been a recurrent theme in discussions of political obligation (and it will be taken up again in Chapter 6); but not all accounts of political obligation in terms of a duty of gratitude rely upon it. Sir David Ross, for example, identifies a *prima facie* duty of gratitude owed generally to those who benefit us. In the context of political obligation he claims that, 'the duty of obeying the laws of one's country arises partly (as Socrates contends in the *Crito*) from the duty of gratitude for the benefits one has received from it' (Ross, 1930, p. 27). The kernel of this conception is briefly stated by one of its critics, A. J. Simmons:

'The gratitude account of political obligation maintains that our receipt of the benefits of government binds us to repay the government because of considerations of gratitude. It maintains further that this repayment consists in supporting the government, part of which support consists in obeying the law' (Simmons, 1979, p. 183).

Unfortunately most references to gratitude as an explanation of political obligation are extremely brief and underdeveloped; and though it has recently been the subject of renewed interest this has been mostly of a critical sort (e.g. Smith, 1973a; Simmons, 1979, Ch. 7).

Much of this criticism has centred on questions about whether the government or polity is an appropriate object of gratitude; whether it has done anything which merits gratitude; whether even if gratitude is appropriate and merited it need take the form of political obligation; or indeed whether gratitude is a duty at all. The gratitude account also seems to be open to the objection concerning unsolicited benefits discussed in the context of the fair-play theory: must we be grateful for benefits which have been imposed upon us? It has, however, also been defended in a sophisticated and developed form by A. D. Walker, who argues that most critics misrepresent the argument from gratitude as resting on a principle of requital or reciprocity; that receipt of a benefit places a person under an obligation to requite the benefactor (Walker, 1988, 1989). Walker, however, reformulates the argument from gratitude in a manner which he claims avoids the objections to this principle. He argues as follows:

'1. The person who benefits from X has an obligation not to act contrary to X's interests.
2. Every citizen has received benefits from the state.
3. Every citizen has an obligation of gratitude not to act in ways that are contrary to the state's interest.
4. Non-compliance with the law is contrary to the state's interests.
5. Every citizen has an obligation of gratitude to comply with the law' (Walker, 1988, p. 205).

As Walker explains, this reformulation of the argument from gratitude does do something to meet the standard objections, but it still leaves many problems unresolved. It also seems worryingly open to exploitation by unscrupulous political powers. However, my principal difficulty with the argument from gratitude, including

Walker's account of it, is that nothing he says persuades me that the kind of obligation he characterises is best understood as one of gratitude.

Walker himself writes that this argument 'suggests a view of political communities as communities whose members are, or should be, bound to one another by ties of goodwill and respect' (Walker, 1988, pp. 210–11). At best, however, this might indicate that gratitude is in some circumstances a part of such ties: it does not suggest that such ties are based on gratitude. Relationships of respect, and even to some extent goodwill, need not imply a duty of gratitude: indeed there would be something almost paradoxical in suggesting that gratitude is the appropriate response to being shown respect. Gratitude may be a more appropriate response to goodwill but it seems too attenuated a basis for political obligation. In short, therefore, while this model of a political community has some attractions, it does not support a defence of political obligation couched in terms of gratitude. However, the development of the positive aspects of such an account must await our later discussion, for it is now time to consider Rawls' second attempt to present a theory of political obligation.

Rawls' duty to uphold just institutions

In *A Theory of Justice* Rawls does not develop the fair-play theory as his account of political obligation, and it is one of the significant departures from his earlier work that he advances instead an explanation in terms of a natural duty to promote and support just institutions. (In fact Rawls distinguishes obligations – which all arise from a principle of fairness – from natural duties; and hence in his use of the term most people do not have any *political* obligations, only natural duties to a just polity. However, I shall ignore this point since the natural duty to promote and support just institutions clearly plays the role of an account of political obligation within Rawls' theory.) His exact statement of the relevant natural duty is as follows:

> 'first, we are to comply with and to do our share in just institutions when they exist and apply to us; and second, we are to assist in the establishment of just arrangements when they do not

exist, at least when this can be done with little cost to ourselves' (Rawls, 1971, p. 351).

While it is possible to see residual elements of the fair-play theory in talk about 'doing our share' in just institutions, this account is significantly different from his earlier theory. Rawls does retain the fair-play theory as a specific partial justification for the political obligation of 'those who have assumed favoured offices or positions, or who have taken advantage of certain opportunities to further their interests' (Rawls, 1971, p. 350); but the details of this exception need not concern us. He explicitly rejects the fair-play account for most people, precisely for the kind of reasons we have already examined. He writes that under the fair-play theory (he calls it the principle of fairness):

> 'citizens would not be bound to even a just constitution unless they have accepted and intend to continue to accept its benefits. Moreover, this acceptance must be in some appropriate sense voluntary. But what is this sense? It is difficult to find a plausible account in the case of the political system into which we are born and begin our lives' (Rawls, 1971, pp. 336–7).

Hence Rawls concludes that a satisfactory account of political obligation, if it is to have general application, cannot depend upon the voluntary acceptance of benefits and he is clear that his revised theory obliges each member of the polity 'irrespective of his voluntary acts, performative or otherwise' (Rawls, 1971, p. 334). Nor in this revised account does political obligation directly derive from a fair distribution of the benefits and burdens of social co-operation; such considerations are encompassed within the theory of justice rather than the account of political obligation. Instead our political obligation arises from a natural duty to support and to promote just institutions.

Rawls is not principally concerned with the issue of political obligation in *A Theory of Justice*; nor has his treatment of it there received much attention from his many commentators. His arguments in support of the claim that we have a natural duty to support and to further just institutions are not especially clear, but they appear to be of two sorts. First, there are the arguments from the inadequacy of other accounts of political obligation, such as his reasons for discarding the fair-play theory. Certainly the conclusions of this book are consistent with Rawls' rejection of fair-play, consent and utilitarian theories, the three other accounts he mentions. However, these arguments can provide only indirect support for his own theory, since the weaknesses of other accounts do not provide positive reasons in its favour. Secondly, there is the argument that the natural duty would be chosen by people in the original position. As explained earlier, the original position is a theoretical construct devised by Rawls to justify basic principles of justice, but it would take us too far from our present purposes to explore this construct in more detail. In any case Rawls' arguments in this context seem to amount to little more than the claim that we need some principle of political obligation, and that the natural duty to support and to further just institutions is preferable to any alternative. However, though Rawls' arguments for his natural duty are not very strong, I do not think this matters. If it can provide a convincing account of political obligation in its own terms this will do much to commend it. I suspect it is more profitable to interpret Rawls' natural duty to support and to further just institutions as a basic moral principle, and to ignore, so far as is possible, its theoretical foundations in his theory of justice. In fact we will not be able to ignore the theory of justice entirely, but that will become an issue in considering the content of the natural duty, and not its foundations. Let us turn, then, to an assessment of his account of this natural duty.

One difficulty for Rawls' new theory is how it encompasses the 'particularity' requirement which, so I have argued, is a necessary feature of any adequate account of political obligation. How, that is, does a general duty to support and promote just institutions bind members to a particular polity, since such a duty would seem to apply to them as persons or moral agents and not specifically as members of this or that particular polity? Of course there are practical or contingent reasons why it is likely to be far easier to support or promote just institutions in the community of which a person is a member. For example, I am called upon to observe the laws of my own community much more often than those of other polities; I can campaign more effectively locally than in a different part of the world; my knowledge and understanding of my own community is likely to be much greater; and I am simply more likely to be involved on a day-to-day level with the institutions and practices of my political community than those of any other. However, such practical considerations would not establish any distinctive duty attached to membership and the general duty would seem to apply equally to supporting or promoting just institutions in political communities other than one's own.

Rawls may appear to circumvent this problem by writing of just institutions which 'apply to us'; the point here seems to be explicitly to distinguish the just institutions of the community of which a person is a member from the just institutions of other polities. Unfortunately it is the apparently *ad hoc* character of this requirement which arouses the suspicions of some of Rawls' critics (Simmons, 1979, pp. 147–52). After all, they continue, is it not more plausible to hold that if there is a duty to support and promote just institutions, this duty is generally applicable: that wherever and whenever one has the opportunity, perhaps subject to the qualification about personal costs, one should support and promote just institutions? However, it is not clear that this criticism is entirely fair to Rawls. His theory of justice is, as he has increasingly emphasised, a theory for a particular society. It is not only that his principles of justice apply within particular societies, but that the method by which they are arrived at is also society-specific. In so far, therefore, as the natural duty to uphold just institutions emerges from the original position, and in so far as the principles are specific to a society, Rawls seems to have some reasons for restricting the scope of this natural duty to the institutions of the society of which one is a member. This reply is at least consistent with his theory, and suggests that his limitation of the requirement of the natural duty to institutions which 'apply to us' may not be as arbitrary as his critics claim. It does, however, imply that this restriction is dependent upon the cogency of Rawls' methodological approach to his theory of justice more generally. In the final analysis the adequacy of this reply is likely to depend in large part on one's overall judgement of Rawls' larger enterprise.

Whatever the merits of this response to the first difficulty, there is a second area of difficulty in his account of the natural duty to support and promote just institutions which relates to the importance of the *justice* of institutions. The problem here is more than that of the endemic disputes about justice mentioned earlier, though the seriousness of that problem should not be underestimated. While Rawls' own theory of justice is supposed to go some

considerable way towards solving that problem, there is an extensive
literature which calls into doubt its success (e.g. Daniels, 1975).
However, leaving aside these doubts, there is also the problem of
where people stand in relation to institutions which do not meet the
criteria of justice. Rawls claims that the natural duty obtains where
institutions are 'just or nearly just', and it is not my intention here to
exploit any possible difficulties in defining what is 'nearly just'.
What of institutions, however, which are not 'nearly just'? Do we
have any political obligations in such circumstances? While the
requirement that one should try to promote just institutions is no
doubt of some help, it does not take us very far in answering this
question, which concerns our response to institutions that are not
nearly just or to institutions that are substantially unjust. It might
seem self-evident that people are under no obligation to support or
comply with unjust institutions, yet there are reasons for doubting
this apparently self-evident conclusion, as I shall go on to explain.

Undeniably there are some institutions so unjust that there is no
decent alternative to a thoroughgoing opposition (though the
personal cost qualification which Rawls inserts might suggest the
reverse, since such institutions are likely to be those which it is most
dangerous to oppose), but there is injustice and yet worse injustice.
As the best is the enemy of the good, so the worst is the enemy of the
bad. Something like this seems to underlie Hobbes' conception of
political obligation; that short of a direct threat to one's life one is
better off under any sovereign than in the state of nature, which is
the only alternative. It is not necessary to accept Hobbes' general
theory, however, to see that there is some truth in the thought that
sometimes it is better to support bad or unjust institutions because
the only realistic alternatives are worse. Of course, this is a view that
needs to be expressed with appropriate caution for it can be, and
often has been, exploited as a specious justification for complacency
in the face of tyranny, but there cannot be any *a priori* argument to
show that such a view is never justified and there is a reasonable
amount of experience to the contrary. For instance, to take a recent
example, in the early years of the Gorbachev regime many Soviet
citizens might well have regarded their society as radically unjust;
they might also have had serious doubts about how far that regime
was willing to take the process of reform; and yet, they could also
have believed that the regime should be supported for all its failings,
because the only realistic alternatives were likely to be worse rather

than better. They might rightly have believed that any more vigorous attempt to promote just institutions would have been counter-productive. Compromise, pragmatism and above all prudence are a necessary part of political morality in a world which does not conform to the moral blueprints of philosophers. Inevitably in practice it may sometimes be difficult to distinguish these virtues from opportunism, timidity or cowardice, but political life, more than most areas of human activity, is not a realm of even near perfection.

A theory of political obligation must address itself realistically to circumstances which are not ideal or nearly ideal, and even to situations which are distinctly morally unappealing. A theory of civil disobedience might do something to fill such a lacuna but the problem is much deeper. In some circumstances we may be morally required to support institutions considerably less than nearly just, yet Rawls' account of political obligation in terms of a natural duty to support just institutions is at best silent, and at worst misleading, on this matter. The force of this observation is further enhanced by the consideration that on Rawls' account of justice (or indeed, according to most theories) few if any states, either present or past, meet the conditions of being nearly just. There is here a point of more general significance. Political philosophy necessarily involves some measure of simplification and abstraction; it cannot accommodate all the rich complexity and nuance of political life. However, this tendency towards abstraction has real dangers to which we need to be alert. What may begin as a laudable attempt to focus on essentials by abstracting from the incidental contingencies of political life may easily degenerate into a philosophically idealised abstraction, bearing at best a very distant and obscure relationship to the world as we experience it. It is this world, not the idealised abstraction of the theorist, which we have to try to comprehend and in which we have to decide how to act. Interestingly enough, this is a point to which Rawls himself seems to have attached increasing importance in his most recent work (e.g. Rawls, 1985). It is also a point of particular relevance to any account of political obligation which aspires to make sense of people's relationship to the polity of which they are actually members.

Leaving aside the specific criticisms of Rawls, however, the conception of political obligation as a natural duty does, I believe, move us closer to a more adequate understanding of political obligation. It needs to be detached from Rawls' theory of justice, and to be revised in other particulars as I shall indicate in Chapter 6. However, before proceeding to that argument, it is necessary to consider one response to the failure so far to come up with any very convincing general theory of political obligation: this is to draw the seemingly obvious conclusion that people do not generally have any political obligations. It may be granted that there are particular instances and circumstances where one or other of the theories is able to provide a more or less convincing justification of a few specific cases of political obligation, but none provides a convincing general account. Perhaps, therefore, for most people political obligation is a chimera. This kind of conclusion seems to have become increasingly commonplace in recent years in the literature discussing political obligation: it is also a central strand in anarchist thought. It is appropriate, therefore, as a preliminary to the positive account of political obligation defended later, to examine the claims of those who deny that (most) people have any such obligations; and in particular to assess the merits of the various forms of anarchism.

5 Anarchism: Political and Philosophical

The three preceding chapters have together considered a wide variety of theories of political obligation and it has been argued that all are, to some considerable extent, unsatisfactory. None of the theories so far discussed provides a convincing general account of political obligation. Inevitably the failure of these theories is likely to give rise to doubts about there being a persuasive general theory of political obligation and it is perhaps not surprising, therefore, that in recent years a number of philosophers have come to more or less sceptical conclusions about the possibility of a philosophically cogent account of political obligation (e.g. Green, 1988; Simmons, 1979, 1987; Smith, 1973a; and Wolff, 1976). Similarly, the perceived failure of attempts to justify political obligation has led to the suspicion that there are few, if any, such obligations and that consequently there is no special moral relationship between people and the polity of which they are members. This is a possibility which is taken most seriously by the differing styles of anarchist thought.

Anarchism and political obligation

For the purposes of discussion in this chapter, anarchism will be considered principally as a theory or doctrine which rejects the possibility of any morally persuasive general theory of political obligation. Anarchism should not be understood as purporting to offer an alternative theory of political obligation, therefore, but rather as rejecting all such theories. It can be seen as a kind of limiting case in the discussion of political obligation. However, for matters are rarely so clear cut, it should be noted immediately that anarchism broadly interpreted does not *necessarily* imply that people do not have any political obligations, though many anarchists would in fact subscribe to such a view; what anarchists reject is any *general* theory or account of political obligation. Some

109

anarchists do advance views which seem consistent with a rudimentary conception of political obligation. Indeed, it is one of the contentions of this chapter that anarchists require something very like an account of political obligation if they are to be able to respond at all convincingly to some of the most common objections to anarchism. At the margins it will have to be allowed that there is some obscurity both about what is or is not to count as a general theory of political obligation and what is a genuinely anarchist view. Anarchism often provokes strongly proprietorial responses among its adherents but the approach adopted here will be catholic rather than exclusionary.

Anarchism, like most moral and political theories, is a rich and internally variegated tradition of thought and ideas and there is perhaps some truth in the claim that 'one of the attractions of anarchism has been the extent to which it has offered something for everybody' (Joll, 1971, p. 213). It is not a simple doctrine the tenets of which can be straightforwardly listed and there are some fundamental divisions and schisms within it. While something of a general nature will be said about anarchism, four rather different forms will be considered more specifically. In the subsequent discussion anarchism is classified into political and philosophical theories; political anarchism is further divided into individualist and communal strands; and philosophical anarchism is divided into positive and negative versions. The purpose of these discussions will be to consider the merits and limitations of the various forms of anarchism as they bear on the problem of political obligation. No attempt, therefore, will be made to provide any comprehensive assessment of anarchism as a political theory, though it is fair to say that the issue of political obligation is at the heart of anarchist concerns. It is an issue addressed by all forms of anarchism and the denial of political obligation has been one of the principal motivating forces of much anarchist thought.

If there is one feature which unites most anarchists, it is opposition to and rejection of the state (though, as will be explained later, negative philosophical anarchists are something of an exception to this and other generalisations about anarchism). As one commentator baldly states, 'opposition to the State is central to anarchism' (Carter, 1971, p. 28). The 'state' is conceived by anarchists as a specific form of political organisation with distinctive properties. David Miller nicely summarises these as follows:

'First, the state is a *sovereign* body, in the sense that it claims complete authority to define the rights of its subjects – it does not, for instance allow subjects to maintain customary rights which it has neither created nor endorsed. Second, the state is a *compulsory* body, in the sense that everyone born into a given society is forced to recognize obligations to the state that governs that society – one cannot opt out of these obligations except by leaving the society itself. Third, the state is a *monopolistic* body: it claims a monopoly of force in its territorial area, allowing no competitor to exist alongside it. Fourth, the state is a *distinct* body, in the sense that the roles and functions which compose it are separate from social roles and functions generally, and also that the people who compose the state for the most part form a distinct class – the politicians, bureaucrats, armed forces and police' (Miller, 1984, p. 5).

Not unsurprisingly, there is some disagreement among anarchists about the extent to which forms of political organisation other than the state are open to similar objections to those made against states, but as a rough rule of thumb the more state-like a political entity the greater the hostility towards it likely to be shown by anarchists. However, it is important to appreciate that few anarchists reject all forms of government or political organisation, and that the vulgar perception of anarchism as the embracing of chaos or disorder is a pejorative parody. Generally, anarchists favour a non-coercive social order and not the absence of any order; that is, a social order without soldiers, policemen, bureaucrats and other functionaries of the coercive apparatus of the state. What, though, is it that anarchists characteristically object to about the state (or state-like entities) and how does this bear on the problem of political obligation?

One kind of objection to the state which is common among anarchists is that it is a harmful and destructive institution. The state is divisive, inegalitarian, punitive, restrictive and anti-social. By 'anti-social' is meant that the state is destructive of those natural social bonds which arise uncoercively through co-operation, mutual respect or affection. For most anarchists these are the bonds which genuinely hold society together and not the laws, threats and institutionalised violence of the state. Most anarchists subscribe to some version of what has been called the theory of spontaneous order:

'the theory that, given a common need, a collection of people will, by trial and error, by improvisation and experiment, evolve order out of the situation – this order being more durable and more closely related to their needs than any kind of externally imposed authority could be' (Ward, 1973, p. 28).

Sometimes this theory is supported by references to seminal historical events such as the early years of the French Revolution and the Paris Commune; at others by invoking the experience of local co-operatives or self-help groups. While these are essentially empirical claims about the relative effects of states and voluntary associations, for most anarchists they have the status of almost self-evident, or axiomatic truths.

Thus it is not the reform of bad states at which anarchists aim since for most anarchists this must be a self-defeating exercise. Rather, what anarchists seek is the end of states: their abolition and not their improvement. Bakunin provides a typically colourful and uncompromising statement of this view:

'It is obvious that freedom will not be restored to humanity, and that the true interests of society – whether of groups, of local organizations or of all the individuals who compose society – will find true satisfaction only when there are no more States. It is obvious that all the so called general interests which the State is reputed to represent, and which in reality are nothing else than the general and continuing negation of the positive interests of regions, communes, associations and the vast majority of individuals subjected to the State, are in fact an abstraction, a fiction, a lie' (quoted in Woodcock, 1977, p. 81).

Inevitably, the plausibility of many of these anarchist claims, even if the empirical accuracy of their characterisation of states is accepted, will depend upon the extent to which the failings of states are open to ameliorative action and, equally importantly, one's view of the likely consequences of possible alternatives. Often at the root of arguments between anarchists and their critics, as with many such disagreements, are differing conceptions of human nature and differing views about what constitute the necessary conditions of a tolerable social life. These are not issues which can be explored in any detail here, and in any case they are not issues which it seems possible to resolve with any finality (Berry, 1986). There is, however, one point which is worth making in defence of anarchism: anarchists need not, and mostly do not, subscribe to the absurdly perfectionist account of human nature with which they are sometimes saddled by their critics. It is true that anarchists generally will be inclined towards the more optimistic end of the continuum of views about human nature, though for many anarchists this applies only to a socialised conception of human nature; but anarchists need not be committed to the view that life in an anarchic condition will be entirely without its disappointments and frustrations. The most the anarchist needs to claim is that human life will be better without the state than with it: there need be no accompanying image of an idyllic utopia in which all conflict is eliminated and human life is perpetually untroubled and serene. However, even granting this point, whether anarchist views of human nature remain too optimistic is an important and unavoidable issue in assessing its merits.

A second type of objection which anarchists make to the state and its institutions, and one which is of particular interest in the context of political obligation, is that the state has no authority over or no right to compel, coerce and otherwise control, its citizens. With the decline of beliefs about the divine right of kings and natural authority more generally, the question arises about what entitles the state or government to command and ultimately to coerce its citizens? Anarchists maintain that the state has no such authority and that the various attempts, such as social contract theory, to show that it does are a sham and a fraud. According to most anarchists the state basically consists of one group of people dominating and coercing another, invariably much larger, group of people. There are, as will be seen later, two versions of this claim. The strongest and most ambitious, associated particularly with positive philosophical anarchism, is the view that the very idea of legitimate political authority is conceptually incoherent. The second and weaker claim is that though legitimate authority is possible, states and state-like institutions cannot possess it because their form is incompatible with the requirements of such authority. In either version, the anarchist challenge to the authority of the state, if successful, would be deeply subversive of any general conception of political obligation.

Before proceeding to a consideration of the four different forms of anarchism identified earlier, it is first necessary to articulate the broad lines of the distinction between political and philosophical anarchism. This distinction basically turns on what follows from the rejection of the authority of the state. Political anarchists are more inclined to view the state as an evil institution which must be destroyed if human beings are to flourish. On their view, not merely do people have no political obligation to their state, they should actively oppose its existence. Philosophical anarchists on the other hand, while denying that states have any distinctive moral authority, do not *necessarily* conclude from this that the state should be abolished. The political implications of philosophical anarchism are much more open-ended. In short, political anarchists are principally exercised by the practical effects of the state, especially its allegedly socially destructive consequences, while philosophical anarchists are more narrowly identified by their denying to the state any claim to moral authority. Inevitably this distinction is somewhat rough and ready, yet it marks a real divide: indeed many political anarchists would reject the claims of philosophical anarchists to be genuine anarchists at all. However, since our concern is not to distinguish the 'authentic' voice of anarchism or to identify true believers this issue will not be pursued further. Rather, our concern will be to consider political obligation in the context of these four strands of thought, and for this purpose nothing of significance will depend upon whether or not they are labelled as 'anarchist'. Anarchism in this context is perhaps best understood as an analytic construct and only incidentally, if at all, as an indication of a specific political commitment.

In any case it would be wrong to exaggerate the affinities even between the different strands of political anarchism. At the extremes individualist and communal anarchism share very little in common other than their antipathy to the state. The positive visions informing them and their underlying assumptions are often radically divergent, and their rival advocates and supporters often intensely hostile to each other. Individualist anarchism is firmly rooted in a belief in the sovereignty of the isolated and independent individual, subject to no moral claims other than a recognition of the similar independence of other sovereign individuals. In contrast communal anarchism is much concerned with social solidarity and mutual dependence. An important aspect of this difference is well brought out by Miller:

'Individualists and communists [communal anarchists] would no doubt agree that their fundamental aim was personal freedom: but whereas individualists would define this negatively, as the absence of interference or coercion, communists would define it positively, as the opportunity to satisfy needs and wants, and claim that, far from one person's freedom being limited by the freedom of others, no one could be really free except in a solidaristic community where each person worked to promote the well-being of the rest' (Miller, 1984, p. 45).

It is principally these differences and the philosophical disagreements which underlie them which necessitate the separate consideration of individualist and communal strands in anarchist thought. I shall begin by considering individualist political anarchism.

Individualist anarchism

Individualist anarchism is marked by its attachment to the independence of the individual. It is a doctrine which developed in the nineteenth century largely as an extreme version of classical liberalism. Classical liberals, though always suspicious of the role of the state, had felt it necessary, at least to some extent, to embrace it as a guarantor of personal liberty, but individualist anarchists have followed through liberal suspicion of the state to its furthest point. Whereas for classical liberals the state was a sometimes necessary evil, for individualist anarchists it was simply an evil. On their view, each person has a right to his or her own life, liberty and property; each may act as they wish without inhibition or restriction provided only that they do not violate the similar rights of others. Again to quote Miller:

'Each person was seen as having an inviolable sphere of action within which he reigned supreme, encompassing both his body and the property he had rightfully acquired. Within the privileged sphere he could act just as he pleased, and moreover he was entitled to give away or exchange anything that fell within it. Thus

people met as sovereign in their own territories. The legitimate
relations between them were those of exchange, contract and gift'
(Miller, 1984, p. 30).

Everybody has a right to defend themselves against unjustified
attack and the only obligations which people have is not to
interfere with each other. Social relations are understood as
essentially similar to economic relations within a free market. Each
person may pursue his or her own ends unobstructed by others;
altruism is permissible but there is no requirement to show any
positive concern for others. This form of anarchism is often rooted
in a doctrine of natural rights which take the form of rights of non-
interference. These rights require us only to refrain from interfering
with others' actions; they establish merely negative duties, and
impose no positive duties upon us to protect, succour, support or
in any way assist other people. It is an outlook often associated
with extreme laissez-faire economics, thoroughgoing moral permis-
siveness, vehement opposition to all welfare legislation and a belief
that any form of compulsory economic redistribution is wicked.
Such a view has been especially prominent in the United States
where it was developed in the nineteenth century by thinkers such
as Lysander Spooner (Spooner, 1966) and Benjamin Tucker
(Tucker, 1893), and its contemporary exponents include David
Friedman (Friedman, 1973) and Murray Rothbard (Rothbard,
1978).

    Individualist anarchism is deeply antithetic to political obligation.
In principle such anarchism is compatible with a voluntary contract
to form a state but not only do individualist anarchists believe that
in fact no states have been based upon a contract, they also
maintain that no sane adult would ever agree to such a contract.
To enter into such a contract would be tantamount to voluntarily
becoming a slave, and this is not an option which would be chosen
by an even minimally rational person. Thus Lysander Spooner
ridiculed the claims of the US government to authority based on
a contract embedded in the Constitution (Spooner, 1966). For the
individualist anarchist a contract is the only possible source of
political authority and the only legitimate basis for political
obligation; but since there is no such contract, there is correspondingly no authority and no obligation. Political obligation is a fraud
perpetrated by governments: there are only individuals with their

rights, and the relationships they voluntarily enter into with each other. The state, and indeed all non-voluntary forms of government, is simply a means by which some people exploit and coerce other people.

The vision of the individualist anarchist is austere and uncompromising but it is also impoverished and neglectful of some basic truths about the human condition and the circumstances of human development. All human beings begin life as vulnerable and entirely dependent, not merely briefly or inadvertently but unavoidably and for many years. Before any human being can become the independent bearer of the right to non-interference of individualist anarchism he or she must be fed, clothed, tended when sick, educated and more generally cared for and nurtured. While much of this will spring from love or good will on the part of parents and those with a sympathetic interest, such good will cannot always be relied upon; either because it may not be present or because it may not have access to the material resources necessary for it to be effective. Furthermore, though such dependence is most extensive and most apparent in infancy and childhood it does not disappear with maturity. None of us can insure ourselves against all of life's contingencies but some adversities and misfortunes may be overcome, or at least their worst aspects mitigated, only by recognising a common predicament and imposing general obligations of aid upon each other. Thus though individualist anarchism rightly recognises as a basic fact that in some straightforward sense we are each of us separate individuals it ignores the complementary truth that we are not self-sufficient beings. Society and social relations are as much a reality as individuality: we experience life through our living with others and we are unavoidably the product, in part, of the culture, practices and social relations within which we are nurtured. The myth of the self-made man is one of the more pernicious deceits of the culture of capitalism. Further, it is wildly implausible to believe that society could ever be intelligible, simply and without remainder, in terms of voluntary contractual relations between separate individuals: language, culture and a whole range of social institutions cannot be so understood. Rather, each of us is born into a complex web of social relations, institutions and practices which contribute to making us what we are, and which cannot all be conceived of as wholly external to a self-sufficient individual with an essence independent of these formative experiences.

It may be asked of the individualist anarchist, therefore, why only duties of non-interference should be recognised as morally compelling? One problem here is that it is notoriously difficult to provide a very plausible derivation of natural rights. There is little agreement among those who have attempted this task and the problems which confront any such undertaking are very considerable. Second, why do we not owe (some) others something, by way of reciprocity at least, for our succour and support? Implicitly, but fundamentally, individualist anarchists tend to rely on institutions such as the family to provide an essential substratum of social life. Yet, even, for example, where parental support for children is entirely voluntary and uncoerced, does it follow that the children acquire no obligations to their parents? Why should it be assumed that some rights of non-interference are 'natural' but not, for example, obligations of gratitude? Individualist anarchism suffers from a peculiarly myopic social vision in this as in other respects. Further, are parents who are not inclined to care voluntarily for their children under any obligation to do so? If the parents cannot be made to do so, does the obligation fall on the community? If the answer to either of these questions is affirmative then there are at least some obligations other than those arising from natural rights to non-interference: if not, then we are confronted with a perspective which will seem to most of us morally repellent. In short, leaving aside the very considerable problems involved in interpreting and justifying natural rights, especially property rights, the moral perspective informing individualist anarchism seems unjustifiably truncated and arbitrary: it neither embraces a consistent amoralism nor a morality rich enough to encompass even the minimal standards of moral concern essential for social life.

These criticisms of individualist anarchists, however, do not show that they are wrong to reject the state or that their denial of political obligation is mistaken. Rather they are intended to cast doubt in a more general way on the coherence and attractiveness of the epistemological assumptions and moral implications of individualist anarchism. They suggest that it is not merely political obligation but ultimately the viability of any sustainable set of social arrangements which are undermined by individualist anarchism. Individualist anarchism inclines towards a picture of human relations which is neither metaphysically nor morally persuasive, implying as it does an essentially atomistic conception of the person. Persons, however, are necessarily social and as such are partly constituted through a social context which cannot be understood simply as a consequence of their prior choices (Taylor, 1985, Ch. 7). However, the same objections cannot be levelled against the alternative form of political anarchism. Communal anarchism is acutely sensitive to the social character of human life. It does not rest on such thoroughgoing assumptions about the sovereignty of the atomistic individual; reciprocity and mutual obligation are an essential part of the communal anarchist's vision and it is to that conception of anarchism we now turn.

Communal anarchism

Communal anarchism is the view associated with the classical anarchists such as Bakunin, Kropotkin and Proudhon and shares much with the socialist tradition of political thought; indeed its proponents are often inclined to see it as the authentic voice of socialist aspirations. Whatever the merits of such a claim, there is one respect in which communal anarchism is clearly distinct from many of the other varieties of socialism. Communal anarchists reject the state and other forms of politically centralised or professionalised control which have been central to much of socialist thought. Historically the division between anarchists and other socialists emerged most clearly in the split between Marx and Bakunin around 1870 and the bitter disputes within the First International which marked both a theoretical and political bifurcation within socialism; a division which continues today (Woodcock, 1963, Ch. 9). Of course many non-anarchist socialists also have favoured the devolution of power and the division is not always a sharp one. Conversely anarchists have been able to appeal to Marx's vision of communist society in *The German Ideology* as one of their inspirations. Initially the dispute was more about means than ends, though increasingly in the twentieth century, beginning perhaps in very different ways with Leninist notions of 'democratic centralism' and Fabian elitism, a socialist tradition has developed in which some form of political centralisation is seen as unavoidable if not always desirable. In this way what began largely as a dispute about the most effective means of instituting a particular form of society about which there was at least notional agreement has developed into a disagreement about the form of society that best represents a desirable and realistic aspiration. The reason many socialists have come to reject the communal anarchist vision of society is that it has increasingly appeared to some of them as utopian, in the pejorative sense of not merely being unrealised but of being unrealisable. This is a point to which we shall return later.

While the spirit informing communal anarchism is very different to that of individualist anarchism, both share a rejection of coercion and a desire to base social organisation upon a principle of free association. Since communal anarchists are inclined to a more benign and co-operative conception of human nature, they believe people will naturally join together to form groups to co-ordinate economic activities and provide mutual aid and support for each other. People are not understood as the atomistic bearers of natural rights so much as mutually concerned and interrelated but independent-minded individuals: in particular communal anarchists reject individualistic anarchists' views about the sanctity of private property. Nor is communal anarchism neglectful of, or necessarily embarrassed by, the fact that individuals grow up within societies and are socialised into the beliefs and practices of their group. For communal anarchists such a process is one of the principal sources of stability within society. However, if people grow up to reject some or most of their heritage then communal anarchists are normally unwilling to license coercion to maintain any particular set of social relations. Society is seen more as a shifting series of common practices and co-operative arrangements to which people voluntarily subscribe and which are subject to continuous renegotiation: relations are basically harmonious, though this does not entirely preclude either diversity or some level of disagreement and conflict.

Communal anarchist conceptions of moral obligation, however, are rather obscure: it is not a subject which receives much emphasis within communal anarchism. There is a tendency for its proponents to subscribe implicitly to some sort of ethical naturalism: they believe that when the oppressive and corrupting influence of the organised coercion of the state is removed, the more naturally co-operative and beneficent aspects of human beings will achieve greater prominence. Anarchists are certainly not unaware of the problems of social co-ordination and anti-social behaviour but they rely on education, custom and emergent voluntary associations to solve these problems. The Russian anarchist, Peter Kropotkin, provides a good example of a communal anarchist's approach to the problem of anti-social behaviour:

> 'Man is a result of those conditions in which he has grown up. Let him grow in habits of useful work; let him be brought by his earlier life to consider humanity as one great family, no member of which can be injured without the injury being felt by a wide circle of his fellows, and ultimately by the whole of society; let him acquire a taste for the highest enjoyments of science and art – much more lofty and durable than those given by the satisfaction of lower passions, – and we may be sure that we shall not have many breaches of those laws of morality which are an unconscious affirmation of the best conditions for life in society' (quoted in Woodcock, 1977, pp. 362–3).

Elsewhere Kropotkin sharply distinguishes custom from law and accepts the need for political organisation, allowing even that it might properly be called 'government', so long as it is naturally emergent from social life (Kropotkin, 1970). For Kropotkin law is an arbitary and coercive imposition of their will by a minority, whereas custom is the coagulation of the spontaneous co-operation among people in response to their common needs. The state is institutionalised coercion, 'government' a natural process of social co-ordination. Furthermore Proudhon, who was more pessimistic about human nature, seems to allow even greater scope for institutions of co-ordination within his conception of 'federation' (Proudhon, 1979). The problem is that these acknowledgements of the necessity for institutional forms of social regulation begin to blur the distinctiveness of communal anarchism: much seems to depend on the contention that custom and other forms of co-operative arrangements are non-coercive. How plausible is this claim?

Coercion and constraint are matters of degree: notions of complete and absolute freedom or pure liberty are incoherent, as some anarchists such as Proudhon have explicitly acknowledged (Proudhon, 1979). In their writings on different forms of social arrangements communal anarchists are more inclined to recognise this than in the rhetoric of their sweeping condemnation of the state. There is, however, a somewhat ambivalent attitude displayed on the question of the extent to which custom and the institutions of social co-ordination must be constraining or coercive (see Ritter, 1980). In response to the common criticism of anarchism that it is utopian and unrealistic, anarchists are inclined to stress, in addition to the positive power of education, the serious consequences of social ostracism, refusal to co-operate and expulsion from the community. Unfortunately, while these features of anarchist forms of social control may rebut the charge of ineffectiveness, they do so at the cost of prejudicing their claim to embody an absence of coercive constraint. If people have little real choice but to observe prevailing customs and to engage in social co-operation on whatever terms happen to exist lest they suffer serious economic and social disadvantage, then the element of voluntary choice is significantly reduced, and the explicit contrast with the coercion of capitalist employers and the state seriously weakened.

Furthermore, much of what we know of small-scale self-regulating communities does not suggest that they are characteristically marked by freedom and diversity, and the anarchist emphasis upon 'education' is easily thought to be sinister in the light of the twentieth century experience of totalitarianism. Nor, in the absence of institutions ensuring fairness and impartiality in the treatment of both complainants and offenders, is one likely to have much confidence in a purely informal system for the investigation, adjudication and arbitration of disputes. It must also be something of an embarrassment to anarchists that most of the many experimental anarchist communities have ended in failure and discord. An inhospitable external environment may do something to explain some of these failures but it is palpably unsatisfactory as an all-purpose excuse for such failures: historical studies of anarchist communities have clearly demonstrated the importance of internal conflicts and disputes in generating fragmentation and dissolution (Miller, 1984, Ch. 11; Woodcock, 1963, Pt II).

There is, therefore, a deep tension at the heart of communal anarchist thinking between a hostility to coercion, the importance of independent judgement and the value of self determination on the one hand, and on the other the recognition that if society is to hold together there will need to be both a widespread moral consensus and very high levels of virtue among the citizenry. Political obligation in such a context is deeply problematic. The idea of a compulsory association making demands of its members is antithetic to the most fundamental convictions of communal anarchists, yet some well developed and fairly demanding conception of 'social' obligation is implied by the positive vision of how an anarchic community might survive and flourish. It is in large part because of this problem that communal anarchists are rarely able, in their positive vision of an anarchist society, to redeem fully the ringing rhetoric which informs their denunciations of political authority when criticising existing practices and institutions.

It is important to recognise that the issue here is not whether some other set of institutions might be preferable to those which currently exist – one would have to be remarkably complacent to believe that no improvement was possible – but whether anarchists can coherently, consistently and realistically do without institutions which exercise authority in ways which are significantly coercive. The burden of the argument in this section has been that they cannot and that this is shown in the work of the classical communal anarchists such as Proudhon and Kropotkin. There is a more or less implicit recognition that social life is impossible without a significant element of coercion: the questions which then arise are not about the need for coercion but about who is to exercise it, for what purposes and subject to what limits? These are the unavoidable issues of political life and equally the concern of political philosophers of whatever political persuasion – of Plato and Hobbes as much as of anarchists. Hence communal anarchists, not withstanding their apparently explicit repudiation of political obligation, seem surreptitiously to reintroduce it, or to rely on surrogates open to similar objections to those which anarchists make against the coercive authority of the state. The approach to political obligation which is likely to be most consistent with the assumptions and values of communal anarchism is some form of voluntarism. Only a voluntarist account is likely to minimise the coercive aspects of political authority which are so objectionable to anarchists. However, this is an approach the defects of which have been considered already, in Chapter 2, and no attempt will be made to recapitulate that discussion. Here, it remains to be seen whether philosophical anarchism fares any better than political anarchism.

Philosophical anarchism

Philosophical anarchists arrive at their conclusions about political obligation by one (or both) of two routes. The first, which might be called justification by default, simply concludes from the failure of all positive attempts to justify political obligation that there is no such obligation. The claim that people are under some form of political obligation needs to be justified; none of the purported justifications is successful; hence, by default, there is no political obligation. This form of philosophical anarchism will be considered more fully shortly. The alternative approach, however, relies not merely on the failure of attempts to justify political obligation, but offers a positive argument of its own as to why there are not, and could not be, any political obligations. The potential superiority of positive philosophical anarchism is obvious. Negative philosophical anarchism is always open to the emergence of some new argument to justify political obligation. Positive philosophical anarchism on the other hand seeks to close off this possibility. Correspondingly, however, the greater ambition of positive philosophical anarchism leaves more scope for a critical response: its defenders have to provide a convincing argument of their own and not merely rely on the argumentative failures of their adversaries. Thus it may be appropriate to think of positive philosophical anarchism as the strong or more ambitious version of philosophical anarchism and the negative approach as the weak or more modest version of this position.

There is some agreement that a view which can be identified as positive philosophical anarchism receives its first explicit and developed formulation in the work of the eighteenth-century utilitarian and anarchist, William Godwin. He held an unusual combination of views, for Godwin believed that the rigorous utilitarianism he espoused issued in anarchist political conclusions. This apparently unlikely conclusion resulted from a highly distinctive feature of Godwin's thought: his claim that although we are each obligated to promote the general happiness, we are all entitled to decide for ourselves whether or not to adopt such an obligation and also free to determine how best to implement it. This is what Godwin calls 'the principle of private judgement' (Godwin, 1976, Bk II, Ch. 6). As has been seen already, some such principle is central to most anarchist thinking but it is fundamental to positive philosophical anarchism. It can be seen, for example, in the most recent and explicitly self-conscious formulation of philosophical anarchism in the work of R. P. Wolff. It is his version which will be treated as paradigmatic and which will be the subject of critical consideration.

In his *In Defense of Anarchism* Wolff argues that any recognition of political authority is inconsistent with the over-riding obligation each person has to act as an autonomous moral agent. As Wolff expresses it:

'The defining mark of the state is authority, the right to rule. The primary obligation of man is autonomy, the refusal to be ruled. It would seem then that there can be no resolution of the conflict between the autonomy of the individual and the putative authority of the state . . . If all men have a continuing obligation to achieve the highest degree of autonomy possible, then there would appear to be no state whose subjects have a moral obligation to obey its commands. Hence, the concept of a *de jure* legitimate state would appear to be vacuous, and philosophical anarchism would seem to be the only reasonable political belief for an enlightened man' (Wolff, 1976, pp. 18–19).

He therefore claims that moral autonomy and political authority cannot be reconciled. He concludes from this that:

'[i]f autonomy and authority are genuinely incompatible, only two courses are open to us. Either we must embrace philosophical anarchism and treat *all* governments as non-legitimate bodies whose commands must be judged and evaluated in each instance before they are obeyed; or else, we must give up as quixotic the pursuit of autonomy in the political realm and submit ourselves (by an implicit promise) to whatever form of government appears most just and beneficent at the moment' (Wolff, 1976, p. 71).

Since 'the fundamental assumption of moral philosophy is that men are responsible for their actions' and since 'moral autonomy is simply the condition of taking full responsibility for one's actions, it follows that men cannot forfeit their autonomy at will' (Wolff, 1976, pp. 12–14) and 'it is out of the question to give up the commitment to moral autonomy' (Wolff, 1976, pp. 71–2). Thus it is the claim to political authority which must be jettisoned. It is important to note here that Wolff is not denying that it may be morally right in some circumstances to do what a state commands, for there may be many morally convincing reasons for so doing which have nothing to do with a state's commanding the action. However, he is denying the claim that the state's commanding something is as such ever a reason for doing what it commands; the philosophical anarchist will not regard laws and edicts as having any moral claim on a person merely because they issue from a state or government, whatever its form or constitution. For the philosophical anarchist, as Wolff bluntly expresses it, 'all authority is equally illegitimate' (Wolff, 1976, p. 19).

Wolff's conception of autonomy is clearly central to his argument and it is therefore necessary to examine it a little more closely. Wolff's approach is broadly Kantian in claiming that

> 'moral autonomy is a combination of freedom and responsibility; it is a submission to laws which one has made for oneself. The autonomous man, insofar as he is autonomous, is not subject to the will of another. He may do what another tells him, but not *because* he has been told to do it . . . That is to say, a man cannot decide to obey the commands of another without making any attempt to determine for himself whether what is commanded is good or wise' (Wolff, 1976, p. 14).

If this were simply the claim that no person can entirely escape responsibility for his or her actions, then there would be little to which exception could be taken. Further, if he were only warning against an uncritical acceptance of the claims of authority, then his exhortation might reasonably be regarded as laudable. Wolff, however, is arguing for much more than either of these innocuous claims. The particular force of his argument from autonomy comes from combining the claim that we have a duty to preserve and enhance our autonomy with the claim that others commanding or requiring us to act in certain ways cannot function as moral reasons for action at all for the autonomous person. For Wolff, being the author of one's actions is not simply a postulate or presupposition of moral agency but is a moral ideal which agents should aspire to realise to the maximum extent possible.

> 'There are great, perhaps insurmountable, obstacles to the achievement of a complete and rational autonomy in the modern world. Nevertheless, so long as we recognize our responsibility for our actions, and acknowledge the power of reason within us, we must acknowledge as well the continuing obligation to make

ourselves the authors of such commands as we may obey' (Wolff, 1976, p. 17).

It is clear that autonomy in this sense is for Wolff the over-riding moral obligation of every person and its systematic pursuit requires denying the claims to authority of any state.

Wolff proceeds to consider and reject various attempts to reconcile moral autonomy and political authority. These will not be discussed here, for if his argument about the nature of authority and autonomy is correct such attempts are necessarily doomed to failure. Though Wolff is not always as clear as he might be about the status of his argument I take it to be primarily an argument about the *logical* inconsistency of autonomy and authority. It is true that this is confused by Wolff's admission that a state based on universal direct democracy would be legitimate, though he also believes it would involve an unjustified surrender of moral autonomy. This admission has led some commentators to assert that Wolff's argument is not really about logical impossibility at all, but more simply and familiarly about the moral undesirability of political authority (e.g. Frankfurt, 1973). However, I shall assume that the argument does attempt to demonstrate the logical impossibility of morally justified political authority, though one that in fact rests upon some highly contentious moral assumptions. This approach seems to accord best with Wolff's own intentions for, as he puts it, 'the arguments of this essay suggest that the just state must be consigned [to] the category of the round square, the married bachelor, and the unsensed sense-datum' (Wolff, 1976, p. 71). He is explicit that reconciling political authority and moral autonomy is not a practical difficulty but a logical impossibility. Clearly if he is right then there cannot be a satisfactory theory or justification of political obligation. Moreover, he is equally candid in drawing attention to the way in which his position is deeply subversive of there being any morally significant sense in which people are members of their polity: he denies that there is any special moral relationship between persons and the political community of which they are members.

'In a sense, we might characterize the anarchist as a man without a country, for despite the ties which bind him to the land of his childhood, he stands in precisely the same moral relationship to

"his" government as he does to the government of any other
country in which he might happen to be staying for a time. When
I [Wolff is a US citizen] take a vacation in Great Britain, I obey its
laws, both because of prudential self-interest and because of the
obvious moral considerations concerning the value of order, the
general good consequences of preserving a system of property,
and so forth. On my return to the United States, I have a sense of
re-entering *my* country, and if I think about the matter at all, I
imagine myself to stand in a different and more intimate relation
to American laws. They have been promulgated by *my*
government, and I therefore have a special obligation to obey
them. But the anarchist tells me that my feeling is purely
sentimental and has no objective moral basis. . . . [M]y obedience
to American laws, if I am to be morally autonomous, must
proceed from the same considerations which determine me
abroad' (Wolff, 1976, pp. 18–19).

This raises important issues some of which will be touched upon
later, but it is the alleged logical inconsistency of authority and
moral autonomy which needs to be examined first for this is the
linchpin of Wolff's argument. It is on the validity of this claim that
the persuasiveness of his argument depends.

     There are two features of Wolff's argument which are especially
open to challenge. First, does moral autonomy have the status of an
over-riding moral obligation as Wolff contends? He does not really
argue for this conclusion but simply asserts that it cannot reasonably be denied. However, this claim seems to exploit an element of
ambiguity in the idea of moral autonomy. The view that we should
take responsibility for our own actions is perhaps unexceptionable,
or at least it will be accepted here. This is not, however, obviously
incompatible with acting on the authority of others, as Wolff
himself at times appears to recognise. In this sense autonomy is a
presupposition of agency and implies only that agents take responsibility for their own actions. It is not an implication of acting on
someone else's authority that one is not choosing to so act or that
one is not responsible for one's actions. The command of an
authority 'determines' the action of the agent only because the
agent decides to follow the command; the agent chooses to act as
the authority requires. As has been frequently pointed out, acting
under someone's authority involves both judgement, that this or

that person has authority, and choice, a decision to act in accordance with what the authority requires (see Winch, 1972a). Neither the faculties of judgement or decision are short circuited when an agent acts in accordance with the instructions of an authority. So in this respect, while Wolff is correct to claim that autonomy is a presupposition of moral action and therefore *qua* moral agent cannot be repudiated, there is nothing in this interpretation of autonomy which is necessarily inconsistent with authority.

However, there is also a second, much richer, interpretation of moral autonomy which Wolff employs in his argument. In this sense moral autonomy is an ideal, a good to be sought in acting and not simply a presupposition of moral agency as such. On this view morality requires us to 'achieve autonomy wherever and whenever possible' (Wolff, 1976, p. 17). It seems to be an ideal rather closer to that advanced by J. S. Mill in his *On Liberty* than to Kant's conception of moral autonomy. Here the concern is very much with living a certain kind of life; one informed by a desire to cultivate one's rational and decision-making capacities to their fullest extent and involving the acquisition of a wide range of knowledge about the options that could be chosen (Raz, 1986). However, while there might be much to commend this form of life there appears to be nothing morally obligatory about such an ideal. It does not seem impossible to live a good life without aspiring to this ideal of autonomy. Furthermore, even if for most of us moral autonomy is a positive ideal, one element of a good life, it is rarely the only component and at least sometimes will not be the dominant one. It will take its place along with other moral ideals, for example having to do with concern for other people, as one of many action-guiding principles which will have to be weighed against these different values in particular contexts. It is highly implausible to think that autonomy will always over-ride values such as not harming other people, supporting loved ones, doing a favour for a friend or even more mundane desires, such as that for a quiet life, with which this ideal of moral autonomy will from time to time conflict.

It may also be asked whether all kinds of authority are necessarily inconsistent with moral autonomy even in this stronger sense? It does not appear that they must be. Certainly a person committed to moral autonomy as an ideal is likely to be generally sceptical of claims to authority but it is not *necessarily* inconsistent with the ideal of moral autonomy to act on another's authority. For example, one way in which one person can acquire authority is by being granted it by another. Suppose Mr X contracts with Ms Y that he will do whatever housework she requires on Tuesday if she will mend his automobile on Monday. If Ms Y repairs the automobile then she has the authority to determine a whole range of Mr X's conduct on the Tuesday. Mr X is required to do the washing, cleaning, dusting and so on as Ms Y commands. Is this a violation of Mr X's autonomy? Surely not – unless one wishes to argue, as Godwin did but Wolff does not, that we should never enter into contracts or make promises. In fact it is hard to see how social life could be carried on if we did not make such undertakings and enter into voluntary agreements which often effectively give one party authority over another. There need be nothing sinister about such relationships and they need not impair an agent's autonomy; indeed in many instances they should rather be seen as expressions of it. It is true, as Wolff claims, that such authority is limited, and I have argued in Chapter 3 that *political* authority cannot be satisfactorily understood as being based upon a contract or promise. However, Wolff's argument, it will be remembered, was that there was a *logical* inconsistency between authority and moral autonomy and this claim is refuted by showing that there are *any* instances of authority which are compatible with moral autonomy.

What, though, of the more specific claim that there is a fundamental incompatibility between *political* authority (under-stood non-voluntaristically) and an over-riding commitment to the ideal of moral autonomy? Even in this case, which is the most favourable to Wolff's argument, matters are not so straightforward as they might appear. As we have seen earlier, Wolff himself concedes that 'there are great, perhaps insurmountable, obstacles to the achievement of a complete and rational autonomy', but he assumes rather than shows that political authority is one of those obstacles which could be removed and is not insurmountable. This is simply to beg the question against those who regard the state, or at least some structure of political authority, as at least a necessary or unavoidable evil, let alone those who argue that it is an essential condition of the good life. There is nothing intrinsic to the view that moral autonomy is an over-riding obligation which dictates that the state or political authority in general must be viewed as an eliminable obstacle to the achievement of that ideal. It might be argued that the state, notwithstanding some element of coercion, provides an essential part of the context within which such an ideal has to be pursued. Again many anarchists are unlikely to believe this but that is because they have other additional moral and empirical objections to the state. At the very least it can be contended with some plausibility that even an over-riding commitment to the ideal of moral autonomy does not, of itself, dictate that political authority must be rejected. Additionally, as has been shown earlier, such an over-riding commitment to the ideal of moral autonomy is in any case far from morally compelling. Indeed, since it is rather implausible to think that it should always be regarded as an over-riding moral obligation, there is little reason to believe that political authority is inconsistent with responsible moral agency. Wolff does not succeed, therefore, in mounting a convincing case for philosophical anarchism on the basis of the alleged contradiction between political authority and moral autonomy. Political authority is not necessarily destructive of moral autonomy, nor need moral autonomy have the kind of over-riding claim on us that Wolff assumes that it must.

However, even if philosophical anarchism cannot convincingly demonstrate its own validity there remains the negative case for it – the justification by default, as I have called it. If none of the arguments purporting to justify political obligation are successful then are we not left with philosophical anarchism as the only available alternative: philosophical anarchism triumphs *faut de mieux*? One preliminary point, though, which should be noted about negative philosophical anarchism is how distant it is in many respects from the concerns of political anarchism. A. J. Simmons, for example, a proponent of negative philosophical anarchism writes:

'We must conclude that citizens generally have no special political bonds which require that they obey and support the governments of their countries of residence. Most citizens have neither political *obligations* nor "particularized" political *duties*, and they will continue to be free of such bonds barring changes in political structures and conventions . . . It is likely that many would find our conclusion (that citizens generally do not have political obligations) objectionable because they believe it to have the following consequence: if citizens do not have political obligations, then they are free to disobey the law whenever they choose. . . . But, from a conclusion that no one in a state has political obligations, *nothing* follows immediately concerning a justification of disobedience. For political obligations are only one factor, among many which would enter into a calculation about disobedience. There are, even in the absence of political obligations, still strong reasons for supporting at least certain types of government and for obeying the law' (Simmons, 1979, pp. 192–3).

This form of philosophical anarchism need share none of the political anarchist's hostility and suspicion towards the state, nor need it endorse the positive commitment to moral autonomy of Wolff. From the point of view of most political anarchists, it is probably true to say that philosophical anarchism does not deserve to be described as anarchism at all. The kind of scepticism towards political obligation shown by the philosophical anarchist, especially the negative philosophical anarchist, is in fact compatible with many very different political commitments (Pateman, 1985, pp. 137–42). While it is of course in principle entirely consistent with political anarchism, negative philosophical anarchism does not necessarily favour it over a wide range of alternative political outlooks. The denial of political obligation need not be especially favourable to scepticism about the value of institutions such as law, government or the state.

The distinctive feature of philosophical anarchism, in either of its two forms, is the denial that there exists any special moral relationship between members or citizens and their polity. The core of this view is

'the conclusion that most of us have no political obligations . . . we are not *specially* bound to obey *our* laws or to support *our* government, simply because they are ours (or because of what their being ours entails). Insofar as we believe ourselves to be tied in some special way to our country of residence, most of us are mistaken' (Simmons, 1979, p. 194).

This is a 'mistake' which needs to be explained, however, for as both Wolff and Simmons recognise this is a conclusion which runs counter to what is widely believed: most people do believe there is a special relationship between them and their polity which distinguishes it from their relationship to other polities. By contrast Wolff and Simmons claim that, in the absence of any convincing moral justification of political obligation, such a belief is mistaken. It is a belief which it is in the interests of government and those in power to foster, but it is not a belief with any justified foundation.

One response to philosophical anarchism therefore is to attempt to show that better sense can be made of the idea of political obligation than that afforded by the traditional accounts which have been subject to such extensive and damaging criticism. Effectively, negative philosophical anarchism offers an invitation to any putative defender of political obligation to provide a more convincing account of it, for the best arguments against negative philosophical anarchism are for the most part arguments in favour of some particular account of political obligation. Negative philosophical anarchism does not show, even if successful, that political obligations do not or cannot exist, but only that the arguments in favour of political obligation do not succeed in showing that most people have such obligations. Perhaps it is particularly worthy of note in this context that the conclusions of philosophical anarchism largely concur with those advanced earlier in Chapter 2 concerning the implausibility of genuinely voluntarist accounts of political obligation. In the next chapter I shall attempt to sketch a more satisfactory account of political obligation which avoids voluntarism and which responds to the challenge of philosophical anarchism. However, there is one general consideration about negative philosophical anarchism which should be examined more closely and which will help to prepare the ground for the positive account of political obligation which follows.

Philosophical anarchism and the polity

Both Wolff and Simmons deny that we have any special bonds in the form of political obligations towards *our* government, state or polity. Whatever obligations we may have towards the law or government apply quite generally; they do not tie us in any specific way to the law or government of the polity of which we are members. However, there is at least a degree of oddness in this claim to which neither Wolff nor Simmons are sufficiently attentive.

This concerns what sense can be made of the claim that a government or polity is *ours* in the absence of some special relationship between us and it. What does it mean to say, for example, that the British government is *my* government? There is something here which needs to be explained but which philosophical anarchism, far from explaining, renders puzzling and mysterious. It may be that some philosophical anarchists (Wolff is a likely instance) would wish to dispense entirely with this way of speaking and thinking. It might be suggested, perhaps following a hint from Wolff, that such a way of speaking manifests only a sentimental illusion. However, it is important to appreciate that it is not *merely* a way of speaking, not merely a form of words, which is at issue because such expressions also embody complex patterns of thought and feeling which are far from insignificant or marginal to our understanding of ourselves and our circumstances. It is a way of thinking which is not obviously or readily dispensable. Of course simply to show that most people share these beliefs and emotions does not, in itself, prove that they are not illusory: political philosophy cannot be reduced to mere opinion polling. However, it should make us reluctant too readily to embrace philosophical anarchism, for negative philosophical anarchism tends to assume that the 'burden of proof' lies with defenders of political obligation, but where a belief is widely shared and deeply implicated in a web of thoughts, feelings and practices there is at least some reason for shifting that burden more towards the sceptic.

More important, though, than where the 'burden of proof' is taken to lie is the issue of what kind of 'proof' this sort of subject matter admits. This, inevitably, is a question which underlies all discussions of political obligation, and is central to moral and political philosophy more generally. It is not a question which can be explored at all fully in this context but it is worth noting that Simmons employs particularly rigorous and demanding standards of moral justification. It would be an interesting exercise, though one that cannot be undertaken here, to apply the same standards of what is argumentatively persuasive to other areas of moral and political philosophy. I have little doubt myself that very few if any moral and political principles and practices are capable of meeting the kind of demanding standards to which philosophers often aspire. Do we have rigorous, logically impeccable and entirely convincing justifications of equality, human rights, personal liberty, the rule of law, the circumstances when war is permitted and so on? It is true that some moral and political philosophers have believed themselves to have effectively settled such questions, but what distinguishes virtually all such claims is that they remain subject to widespread and persistent dissent and controversy. It seems empty at this point to invoke once again the claim that the validity of an argument is not determined by the number of its adherents. This must be granted; but such an observation only helps to *define* the problem, not to resolve it. Even allowing for high levels of irrationality, ignorance, self interest and such like, all of which it would be reasonable to discount, the level of philosophical agreement even between competent and similarly trained and educated political philosophers is remarkably low (Rorty, 1989). This is an important fact about political philosophy, and one of which any conception of what political philosophy is about and what it can reasonably hope to achieve needs to take account.

A second possible response to the question of what sense can be made of the claim that a government or state is *ours* would be to offer an explanation of this which dispenses entirely with notions of political obligation. This may be possible but it is not easy to see how; nor have any negative philosophical anarchists attempted such an explanation. At the very least this would require some creative philosophical work on the part of negative philosophical anarchists. In the absence of such accounts it is difficult to offer a prognosis about their likely success but it certainly does not seem that such a task will be straightforward.

What these considerations suggest is that the fundamental challenge of negative philosophical anarchism lies in its subversion of political relationships through undermining the shared understandings which are constitutive of such relationships. In short it is mistaken to think, as critics and defenders alike have tended to assume, that political life is left more or less unchanged by dispensing with some conception of political obligation and adopting the perspective of philosophical anarchism. Unless it can be shown that we can continue to talk intelligibly and credibly of *our* government or *our* state, then a radical rethinking of our political relations is an unavoidable consequence. Of course, as has already been indicated, such a conclusion need not imply a criticism of philosophical anarchism but it does suggest, what most political anarchists have always proclaimed, that we cannot reject political obligation and pretend that we can carry on pretty much as before. Perhaps a more rigorous thinking through of the consequences of embracing philosophical anarchism will lead back towards some form of political anarchism, though that is not the only possibility. For example, if we accept that 'all political authority is equally illegitimate' then it might paradoxically encourage a more acquiescent attitude to state power.

All forms of anarchism are a challenge to political obligation and, as such, a challenge to fundamental aspects of our understanding of political life. This challenge may be uncomfortable but it cannot be refused simply for that reason. In this chapter I have tried to examine the nature of that challenge and to explore some of its more significant implications. Only occasionally have I attempted to decisively refute anarchist claims: as I have indicated, arguments in political philosophy rarely permit such certainty. However, I have sought to show that the anarchist challenge to political obligation is not without serious difficulties of its own. The strategy employed has been, for the most part, to undermine and render more manageable the anarchist challenge rather than attempt to show that it is demonstrably erroneous. Inevitably any full response to that challenge must include a more positive account of political obligation, and it is to that I turn in the next chapter.

6 Political Obligation Reconsidered

The problem of political obligation as it is interpreted here concerns the grounds, limits and content of the obligation of people to the polity of which they are members. In the context of a political community it is concerned with who is obligated to whom or what and under what conditions. The principal philosophical task has been understood to be to discover or construct a convincing moral justification for the political obligation of members to their polity. In the preceding chapters several such attempts have been assessed and, to varying degrees, found wanting. None of them provides very plausible reasons for attributing political obligations to most members of any polity that does exist, has existed, or indeed, is likely to exist. The claim has to be expressed in this rather qualified way because some of the arguments do justify some political obligations for a few people under some actual, or for more people under some highly unlikely, circumstances. The point is that they do not provide what they have mostly sought, which is a satisfactory *general* justification of political obligation. Further, one class of responses to this failure, the various forms of anarchism, has also been considered and doubts expressed about its adequacy. However, a very different kind of response to the perceived failure of justifications of political obligation has been advanced by proponents of what I shall call, following Carole Pateman, 'the conceptual argument' (Pateman, 1973). These philosophers infer from this failure that there is something philosophically misconceived about the very enterprise of trying to offer a general justification of political obigation (MacDonald, 1951; Rees, 1954; McPherson, 1967; and Pitkin, 1972).

The conceptual argument

Whereas anarchists appear to resolve the problem of political obligation by explaining away the *obligation*, proponents of the conceptual argument are frequently accused of resolving it by explaining away the *problem*. For, under the influence of certain tendencies associated with the later philosophy of Wittgenstein, and often also a degree of complacency about the merits of liberal democratic forms of government, it has been denied that there is any general problem of political obligation. The claim embodied in the conceptual argument is that the problem of political obligation, understood as the search for a general justification of it, is a pseudo-problem, the result of conceptual confusion. Despite some significant differences in the way in which this argument has been developed, its conclusion is that any attempt to provide grounds for, or supply a justification of, political obligation in general is misconceived.

This conclusion rests on the contention that the concepts of state, government or political authority (and these are often not distinguished), on the one hand, and the concept of political obligation, on the other, are logically or conceptually connected. Thus, it is argued, there is a fundamental confusion in supposing that the former could exist without the latter, and since this is just what those who seek a general justification of political obligation do suppose, their project is fatally undermined. This project presumes that state, government or political authority might exist without any corresponding obligation, and that therefore some further account of the source or moral justification of political obligation is essential. However, according to the proponents of the conceptual argument, there is a logical relationship between state, government or political authority and political obligation, and therefore the attempt to provide some kind of independent justification of the latter is neither necessary nor possible. Some care, though, is needed in presenting the conceptual argument, for it is emphatically not part of the argument, for example, to deny the possibility of justifying obedience (or disobedience) to this or that particular law or government. What *is* denied is that there can be any general justification of political obligation and, in trying to elucidate this claim, it is necessary to look in more detail at some of the arguments that have been adduced in its defence.

Probably the earliest statement of the conceptual argument is to be found in a paper by Margaret MacDonald in which she writes:

'A general proof of the existence of material objects seems impossible, and to ask for it absurd. No general criterion of all right actions can be supplied. Similarly the answer to "Why should I obey *any* law, acknowledge the authority of *any* State, or support *any* Government?" is that this is a senseless question. Therefore any attempted reply to it is bound to be senseless, though it may perform other useful or harmful functions. It makes sense to ask "Why should I obey the Conscription Act?" or "Why should I oppose the present German Government?" because by considering the particular circumstances and characteristics of all concerned, it is possible to decide for or against obedience and support. We all know the kind of criteria according to which we should decide these issues. But although it looks harmless and even very philosophical to generalise from these instances to "Why should I obey *any* law or support *any* government?" the significance of the question then evaporates. For the general question suggests an equally general answer, and this is what every political philosopher has tried to give. But no general criteria apply to every instance. To ask why I should obey *any* laws is to ask whether there might be a political society without political obligation, which is absurd. For we mean by political society, groups of people organised according to rules enforced by some of their number' (MacDonald, 1951, pp. 183–4).

This passage, and indeed the whole argument, which is very briskly presented, is not easy to interpret or assess and in the following discussion a number of claims and issues that might reasonably be thought highly contestable will be ignored. A crucial part of the argument is the comparison of the request for a general justification of political obligation with that for a general proof of the existence of material objects. In relation to the latter, the argument appears to be that a demonstration of the existence of any particular material object will necessarily presuppose a background within which the existence of some material objects is not doubted. Comprehensive scepticism is unintelligible because one cannot demonstrate the existence of material objects in general; and thus to think that, lacking such a general proof, their existence is doubtful, is absurd.

Whatever the merits of this view, and there is an extensive and sophisticated philosophical literature concerning scepticism, it is difficult to see how the argument can be analogously developed in the case of political obligation. In part at least, this difficulty arises because what is sought by someone wanting a general justification of political obligation is a particular moral argument and not a justification of morality as such. It is the latter which might more reasonably be thought to parallel the demand of the sceptical epistemologist for a general proof of the existence of material objects. MacDonald claims that, in dealing with the problem of political obligation, 'the political theorists want an answer which is always and infallibly right, just as the epistemologists want a guarantee that there are material objects', and that both are 'equally senseless requests for they result from stretching language beyond the bounds of significance' (MacDonald, 1951, p. 184). Whether or not this is so, the analogical basis of this argument remains rather obscure and underdeveloped and does not succeed in establishing MacDonald's claim.

Where MacDonald's argument is clearest the objection to general theories of political obligation seems, much more straightforwardly, to be that no such theory can do justice to the complex considerations involved in deciding, on any particular occasion, whether or not obedience to a law is justified. Whereas general theories 'seek to reduce all political obligation to the application of an almost magic formula', it is simply impossible to provide comprehensive and precisely formulated criteria for when a law should oblige (MacDonald, 1951, p. 185). This seems a less than sensitive account of what most theories of political obligation have been about; and in any case seems very different from the objection to attempts to provide a general proof of the existence of material objects. There the impossibility seemed to lie not in the complexity of the considerations but in the unintelligibility of doubt. What the conceptual argument requires is an equivalent to the latter in the case of political obligation. Nevertheless, though MacDonald's argument cannot be judged convincing, the questions she raises about what can be expected of a theory of political obligation are legitimate and searching. In particular, her emphasis upon the variety and complexity of considerations affecting practical political judgments suggests the inevitable limits of any philosophical account of political obligation. However, this is a point which can also be accepted by those who reject the conceptual argument, and may provide independent reasons for scepticism about the possibility of a general philosophical theory of political obligation. As John Dunn has written:

'the prospects for a theory of rational political obligation as this has generally been conceived are beyond hope, not because (as has sometimes been supposed) there is nothing for such a theory to be about, but there is so much that such a theory *has* to be about (so much to which it *has* to do justice), if it is to stand a chance of proving valid' (Dunn, 1980, p. 299).

This conclusion is similar to MacDonald's that 'as rational and responsible citizens, we can never hope to know once and for all what our political duties are' (MacDonald, 1951, p. 86), but it has no connection with her other arguments. It is, however, a problem which any theory of political obligation needs to take into account, and it does indeed impose limits on what we should reasonably expect from any general philosophical account of political obligation.

A more recent and much fuller version of the conceptual argument is that developed by Thomas McPherson. In a crucial summarising passage he writes:

'That social man has obligations is therefore not an empirical fact (which might have been otherwise) that calls for an explanation or "justification". That social man has obligations is an analytic, not a synthetic proposition. Thus any general question of the form "Why should we accept obligations?" is misconceived. "Why should I (a member) accept the rules of the club?" is an absurd question. Accepting the rules is part of what it *means* to be a member. Similarly, "Why should I obey the government?" is an absurd question. We have not understood what it *means* to be a member of a political society if we suppose that political obligation is something we might not have had and that therefore needs to be justified' (McPherson, 1967, p. 64).

McPherson, like MacDonald, does not deny that particular obligations may stand in need of justification or that on occasion they may not be justified. Rather, his claim is that:

'What it does not make sense to ask for justification of is the existence of *obligations in general*, for that we are involved in obligations is analytically implied by membership of society or societies. . . . We may wonder whether the government is right to require this or that of us, but we cannot (logically cannot) dispute that membership of political society involves obligations to government' (McPherson, 1967, pp. 64–5).

It is true that McPherson occasionally equivocates between this view, that it does not make sense to ask for a general justification of political obligation, and the clearly incompatible view that such a general theory is possible but that 'it would have to be (against the protests of theorists of the past) an eclectic one. Although no theory provides the whole answer, each of them might provide perhaps some part of the answer' (McPherson, 1967, p. 52). It might properly be asked how even an eclectic theory could possibly provide a satisfactory answer to an 'absurd question'. But, despite these and other ambiguities in the formulation of his argument, it is tolerably clear that McPherson's intended claim is that the enterprise of seeking a general justification of political obligation rests on a conceptual confusion and is, therefore, radically misconceived.

A more genuine and deeply rooted difficulty in McPherson's presentation of the conceptual argument, and one that has received much emphasis from his critics, is that it is unclear whether the argument is supposed to apply exclusively to modern liberal democracies or more widely. He writes in his Introduction that 'most of what I say in this book is intended to apply to modern liberal democracies – more particularly to modern Britain. Some of what is said is, of course, capable of a much wider application' (McPherson, 1967, pp. 2–3). Unfortunately, McPherson never consistently distinguishes that which applies only to 'modern liberal democracies' from what is 'capable of a much wider application'. As a result Carole Pateman, for example, has inferred that the conceptual argument is intended to apply only to liberal democratic polities. She objects to this, claiming that:

'Any argument that moves straight from the conceptual connection between "being a member of political society" and "political obligation" to conclusions about our obligations to specific institutions is stretching purely conceptual analysis beyond its proper limits. To argue from "being a member of a political society" directly to "having a political obligation to the (liberal democratic) state" is to make the implicit assumption that "political society", "government" and "the state" all imply each other and that there is a logical, not just an empirical connection, between the notions of political society and the state' (Pateman, 1973, pp. 223–4).

The substance of this argument is surely correct. If the conceptual argument is limited to liberal democracies, this must be through an unargued identification of the polity or 'political society' with liberal democracy. Though such a case could be argued, McPherson does not do so, and it is much more doubtful whether it could be argued with any persuasiveness. As it stands, the limitation of the conceptual argument to liberal democracies appears arbitrary and unjustified.

A second aspect of McPherson's argument which has given rise to serious objection, and which distinguishes his view from that of almost all recent philosophers, is his denial that political obligation is moral in character. Rather, he maintains, political and moral obligations are distinct species of the genus obligation. Unfortunately, it is much easier to see what political obligation is not, on this account, than what it is. Political obligation is not legal obligation, for the two are explicitly distinguished by McPherson, nor is it straightforwardly prudential obligation (McPherson, 1967, pp. 77–8, 26–7). More particularly, political obligation is neither moral in character nor subordinate to moral obligation, for McPherson is particularly concerned to point out that 'the kind of moralising politics that I am objecting to is the kind engaged in by philosophers who attempt to subordinate political principles to moral' (McPherson, 1967, p. 82). What political obligation is, however, remains, stubbornly mysterious. This is, nevertheless, an issue worth pursuing because McPherson's reasons for denying that it is moral relate to some wider questions about political obligation.

His first reason for denying that political obligation is moral raises an issue that has already been discussed in connection with voluntarist theories. He writes:

'We should, I think, generally be reluctant to use the expression "moral obligation" for a duty not voluntarily assumed. Some cases covered by the expression "political obligation" by contrast are certainly cases where we have obligations that we have not voluntarily assumed' (McPherson, 1967, p. 70).

Thus his first argument, which has a familiar ring to it, seems to be that, since all moral obligations are voluntarily assumed and some political obligations are not, it follows that political obligations cannot be moral obligations. McPherson's second argument also has to do with an alleged difference between the moral and the political for, while the former is 'concerned with personal relations', the latter concerns 'our relations to the state and it to us', (McPherson, 1967, p. 74) and what is appropriate for personal relations may not be appropriate in our relations to the state. Thus he claims that 'certain kinds of behaviour are looked upon as not falling within the sphere of morality at all. The question as people see it is whether they are politically right 'or wrong . . . and this seems to them just a different question to the moral one' (McPherson, 1967, p. 78). Thus, at least in part, his thought seems to be that the sphere of moral obligation is that of personal relations, while political obligations are concerned with relations between individuals and particular kinds of institutions (McPherson, 1967, p. 81). This second point also seems to suggest that people simply do not morally judge political actions. However, while it may be true that political morality will have some distinctive features which distinguish it from personal morality, the claim that political actions are not (or cannot be?) subject to moral appraisal seems so obviously mistaken that I shall ignore it.

McPherson is, I think, wrong in construing either of these arguments as reasons for denying that political obligation is moral in character. However, though the use he makes of these arguments is mistaken, they do reveal important features of any adequate account of political obligation. First, he is correct in arguing that political obligation is not usually voluntarily assumed, but wrong in thinking that this distinguishes it from moral obligations, since not all moral obligations are voluntarily assumed. When discussing voluntarist theories in Chapter 2, we saw that some moral obligations are neither chosen nor the consequence of people's choices. Secondly, McPherson is right in recognising that a satisfactory account of political obligation may differ significantly from any account that could be given exclusively in terms of obligations deriving from personal relations without any reference to their institutional setting. However, he is mistaken in believing that this distinguishes political from moral obligations, for many moral obligations, too, are incomprehensible without reference to social institutions. For example, loyalty to the office of the vice-chancellor within a university is distinct from loyalty to the particular person who happens to occupy that position, but both are undeniably moral qualities, even though the former inextricably depends upon social institutions. Overall, therefore, neither argument provides a convincing reason for denying what has usually been thought uncontroversial – that political obligation is a species of moral obligation.

These criticisms of McPherson's argument seriously compromise its validity. However, some of the substance of the conceptual argument can, I believe, be reformulated in a manner which avoids these objections to his presentation of it. The core of this argument, as I shall interpret it, is that having political obligations is part of what it means to be a member of a political community. Furthermore, despite McPherson's misleading references to clubs, which immediately bring to mind the picture of the political community as a voluntary association, membership of a polity is not generally the result of a voluntary undertaking to join. This, at least, is the kernel of the conceptual argument which will be preserved and elaborated in my own account of political obligation. However, it is important to recognise that such an elaboration is required and that it is insufficient merely to assert that being a member of a polity simply means having a political obligation without further explanation. What has been found puzzling about political obligation needs to be examined and not dismissed. It is this task which will take up the remainder of this chapter.

Political obligation and the family

The comparison of the polity with the family has, as was mentioned in Chapter 4, a long history, dating back at least to Socrates. It has, however, with a few exceptions, fallen into disrepute among political philosophers and many would agree with A. J. Simmons' comment that, 'at least since Locke's *Two Treatises* it has been widely accepted that the purported analogy between political and familial relationships is something less than compelling' (Simmons, 1979, p. 162). While not denying that there are many important disanalogies, I believe such a comparison can help to illuminate political obligation in ways that its cursory dismissal may overlook. In particular, I shall suggest that familial obligations share several features with political obligations, and that the family provides a good example of a context in which obligations are experienced as genuine and rather open-ended, and are not the result of a voluntary undertaking. Moreover, having such obligations is ordinarily part of what it *means* to be a member of a particular family. Thus, while the specific obligations which are part of family life are not closely analogous to political obligations, they do, I shall suggest, provide a helpful comparison for its understanding.

Before developing this comparison, however, it is first necessary to warn against a possible misunderstanding. Historically, analogies and comparisons with the family have often been introduced into discussions of political obligation to support patriarchal or paternalist accounts of political relationships. This is clear, for example, in seventeenth-century comparisons of paternal and political authority which model the latter on the authority of the father (Schochet, 1975). Recent feminist theory, moreover, has enlarged our understanding of patriarchy and also radically reinterpreted its historical significance (e.g. Pateman, 1988, 1989). However, analyses of political obligation which invoke the family as an analogy need not have paternalist or patriarchal implications, and I hope that nothing in the argument which follows depends upon such assumptions.

The family is a context in which we commonly acknowledge obligations which are not self-assumed in the way that, for example, obligations arising from promises are; for mutual obligations exist within the family which cannot be explained in terms of individual choices or voluntary undertakings. While it could at least be argued that the obligations of spouses, both to each other and to their offspring, are the result of voluntary commitments on each of their parts (a claim which is itself more than doubtful in the case of parental obligations to their offspring), it is clear, for instance, that the obligations of siblings to each other and of sons or daughters to their parents, cannot be similarly explained. The relationships in which we find ourselves with parents and siblings are not ones we have chosen, and not having chosen our family is not a reason for denying that we have obligations to them. The difference between such obligations and those arising from promises or consent are worth making a little more explicit. If an obligation is claimed to arise from a promise or from consent, it is a decisive objection to such a claim that no promise was made or no consent given. This is, in another context, the familiar objection to contract and consent theories of political obligation. However, there is nothing equivalent to a promise or consent in the case of people's obligations to their parents and siblings, yet there *are* obligations. Nor is it very plausible to claim that these obligations are satisfactorily explained in terms of some supposedly fair distribution of familial burdens and benefits. For it would be a distortion even of our obligations to our parents, to assume they are appropriately explicable in terms of some calculation of the balance of cost and benefit. Furthermore, such moral book-keeping cannot usually even purport to explain the obligations that hold between siblings. Nor again are these obligations necessarily parasitic upon the presence of particular personal feelings or emotions, for they obtain in the absence of love, or any feelings of personal warmth, and may indeed be felt more keenly as a result. I do not intend to suggest that some of these considerations may not properly influence an individual's view of what these obligations require or their stringency, but they do not provide a general moral justification of them. Moreover, while gratitude may do something to explain the obligations of people to their parents, it is at best only a partial explanation. Other people may help us more than our parents, and we may, therefore, incur an obligation of gratitude to them; but we do not characteristically think of that obligation in the same way as we think of our obligations to our parents, nor would we believe that gratitude was an appropriate common currency by which to measure their value. Similarly, gratitude does not appear to be a very plausible explanation of obligations between siblings.

For most people and in most circumstances obligations of family membership need no justification in terms of some external moral principle or some obligation-creating voluntary undertaking. It is generally sufficient to point out that one does stand in a certain relationship to this or that member of one's family. Why must there be a further moral justification? Indeed the very demand for justification may itself be thought odd and out of place. If, to cite a trivial example, I am asked to go to a party one evening and I reply I cannot because it is my parents' silver wedding anniversary and I must spend the evening with them, though I had not promised to stay with them and I would prefer to go to the party, then frequently no more needs to be said. If I were then asked why this was a reason for not going to the party we would mostly find the question odd and inappropriate. What more does the questioner think needs to be supplied? Even if more is said about why my parents' silver wedding matters, and the nature of family life, it would be unlikely to have anything to do with contract, consent, fair-play or the maximising of utility, and even gratitude need not figure in such an account. It would most likely involve spelling out what is involved in familial relations, at least as understood within a particular conception of family-life, rather than referring to any general moral principle. Such obligations 'derive' from membership of a family and it is in terms of what this means that they have to be understood.

It is one of the pervasive deforming features of much modern moral philosophy that no obligation can be recognised and no moral requirement admitted which has not been justified from first principles. Yet it can be argued, and increasingly has been by such very different philosophers as Alasdair MacIntyre, Richard Rorty, Bernard Williams and Peter Winch, that the aspiration to rationally justify all our moral beliefs and practices in this way is neither necessary nor possible (MacIntyre, 1981; Rorty, 1989; Williams, 1985; Winch, 1972b). This is a point to which we shall return later, but in the present context it is enough to say that it is our recognition of particular kinds of relationship and the claims which they make on us which explains the mutual obligations involved in familial life. Of course, the content of such obligations will vary with the form and structure of family life, both between cultures and through time, but where there are families, there will be obligations between its members. It is part of our understanding of what it is for some group to be a family that there be some such obligations.

Before proceeding to a comparison with political obligation, two objections to what has been said about familial obligations must be considered. First, it might be argued that the above account of familial obligations, even if true, applies only to young children, less than fully responsible for their actions, and that the particular problems they present differ from those confronting mature and responsible adults. However, this objection would misconstrue my argument, for the 'children' in it are indeed mature adult human beings. (It is only when people have attained a certain level of intellectual and moral development that we can sensibly speak of them as having moral obligations.) People do not cease to be sons or daughters, or brothers or sisters, on reaching a particular age. Familial obligations do not end at the age of puberty or majority or with the departure from the family home, though such relationships most certainly undergo changes with the passage of time and the growth of children into adulthood. The important point for this argument, however, is that these familial obligations are not specific to 'childhood'.

The second objection is more serious and substantial, though less easy to formulate. In essence it charges the kind of account which has been offered with sentimentality about the family: it is claimed that actual families often bear little relation to such an overly-moralised account of them. However, it is not easy to see why the fact that members of families often behave appallingly to each other – cruelly, selfishly, greedily, callously and so on – is any more of an embarrassment to this account of familial obligations than, for example, the facts of lying, cheating and dissimulation need be to an account of the morality of promising. Familial obligations, like much of morality, may be acknowledged in the breach as well as in the observance. Moreover, as I mentioned earlier, such obligations may be felt especially keenly when the appropriate emotional support is lacking. In any case, given my concern to develop a comparison with political obligation, it is important that the role of conflict and power relations within the family should not be unduly minimised, for no one is likely to be tempted to forget their importance within a polity, however rose-tinted or soft-centred their view of the family.

There is also one further potential misunderstanding, of a more general sort, which should be laid to rest. Reference will regularly be made to recognising or acknowledging obligations of membership, whether it be of a family or a polity. This is not, however, as some might imagine, to reintroduce consent or some other voluntarist element through the back door. Acknowledging or recognising our obligations does not imply that some act of acknowledgment or recognition creates the obligations. The obligation of a man to his brother, for example, does not arise from a voluntary undertaking, and in this respect is quite different from his obligation to pay someone else five pounds, because he promised to do so. The man acknowledges his obligations in both cases, but this acknowledgement has nothing to do with how those obligations arose or their moral basis. All moral obligations and duties must be acknowledged or recognised if an agent is to act upon them, but this leaves entirely open the question of how any particular obligation is to be explained or justified. However, we should return now to the comparison between the family and the polity.

Individuals are most often born into a polity as they are born into a family, and the obligations they acquire are often somewhat indeterminate. Membership of a polity is rarely optional and, where it is, it may be so only by courtesy of that polity: it is normally acquired simply by being born into a political community and is frequently sustained through continued residence within its territory. These are the conditions which standardly characterise membership. Of course, there are many relevant phenomena which cannot be accounted for in quite this way; such as resident aliens, stateless persons, dual citizenship, naturalisation and so on, just as the familial case is complicated by facts of abandonment, divorce, adoption and so on. However, though these are significant complications, and some account of them would need to be given in any more comprehensive discussion, they are comparatively marginal and need not seriously impinge upon the argument here. This argument is concerned with what is best thought of as the standard, or paradigmatic, case of membership of a polity, and it would be as mistaken to base any general account of that on, for example, naturalisation, as it would be to base any general account of the family on adoption. Moreover, at this level of abstraction, as with the family, only the broad contours of the obligation can be sketched. The obligations cannot be given much specific content and are inevitably characterised in rather general terms. A more detailed specification of the content of political obligation is possible only in the context of an enquiry into the particular features of a given political community.

In developing my account of political obligation, I shall continue from time to time to explore and draw on the analogy between a family and a polity, but it is equally important to recognise the limits of this comparison. My claim is that a polity is, like the family, a relationship into which we are mostly born; and that the obligations which are constitutive of the relationship do not stand in need of moral justification in terms of a set of basic moral principles or some comprehensive moral theory. Furthermore, both the family and the political community figure prominently in our sense of who we are; our self-identity and our understanding of our place in the world. There are, however, several disanalogies between the polity and the family, at least two of which should be explicitly acknowledged as of particular importance. First, a family involves a structure of essentially personal relations whereas the polity does not. One aspect of this difference relates to the distance between the role and the person. While in the context of the family I can for some purposes distinguish the role from the person – I can, for example, respect this person as my father but not as a man – the connection is a peculiarly close one. 'My father' is in a fundamental respect tied to the particular person who is my father: it is not for example a role that can have a succession of short-term occupants and remain meaningful. Our understanding of the polity, government and such like is usually not tied to particular specific persons in this way.

The second, and probably more significant disanalogy concerns the place of coercion. One reason for using this analogy has traditionally been to claim that political authority is importantly similar to parental authority with respect to the power of coercion (Filmer, 1991). On this view the political authority of the magistrate, the civil power, is similar to that of the father over his children. However, in this repect the analogy is inappropriate since it depends upon treating people as if they were young children. The way in which I have been regarding familial obligations eschews any such assimilation, and the account of political authority must be significantly different from that of parents over their young children. The kind of familial obligations to which I have referred do not involve any systematic claims about the authority of one member of a family over another. Political obligation, on the other hand, is in part constituted by the acknowledgement of some claim to coercive authority. It is additionally this aspect of political obligation which has typically been thought to make it so morally problematic. It is now time to provide a fuller exploration of the meaning of a specifically political obligation.

Identity and political obligation

A member of a polity is uniquely related to that polity and it is this relationship which it has been suggested is best understood as one of political obligation. It is, however, important to understand the kind

of relationship that this involves. As Rush Rhees in his discussion of
the relationship between the citizen and the state writes:

> 'The "relation" seems to be an internal one, not like my relation
> to the park when I am in it. When I am not in the park, this will
> make no difference to the park or to me. But we cannot think of
> the state without thinking of individual citizens or vice-versa. But
> neither is "the relation of the individual to the state" at all like
> "the relation of the individual wolf to the pack" or "the relation
> of the individual to the crowd". These could be understood as
> quasi-physical relations and the relation of the individual to the
> state is not that. It has rather to be studied, apparently, in terms of
> obligation' (Rhees, 1969, pp. 81–2).

Rhees' point here is an important one. Being a member of a polity is
not simply a matter of living in a particular geographical area, even
though the facts of one's place of birth and residence, as I have
indicated, play an important role in our acquiring political obligations. Nor is being a member of a polity simply a matter of living
with a particular group of people, though that too has some place in
explaining our political obligations. Being a member of a polity
involves a specific moral relationship which needs to be distinguished, on the one hand, from duties to friends, colleagues and
family and, on the other, from entirely general moral requirements
such as charity and non-maleficence. In terms of its range of
application political obligation is more extensive than the former
but less so than the latter. It extends so far as, but no further than,
the limits of the political community of which one is a member.

Perhaps it is possible to begin to make a little clearer what is
involved in membership of a polity by being a little less abstract.
The existence of this relationship between member and polity
shows itself in many and various ways, but one of the more
interesting and important is that we view the actions of the polity
of which we are members, *our* polity, in distinctive ways. I do not
mean that we need have especially harsh or indulgent standards by
which to judge its actions but rather that, whether or not we
approve of them, its actions appear to be particularly connected to
us. And this connection is to be located not so much in our
judgement of their consequences as in our sense of their author-
ship. For there is an important, though limited, sense in which we

understand ourselves as the authors of such actions, even when we oppose them: they are the actions of our polity, the polity of which we are members. They are actions performed in our name and, as members of the polity, we are related to *its* actions in a way that we are not to those of polities of which we are not members. This is the kind of relationship expressed, for instance, in the comments of the Polish film director Krzysztof Kieslowski in reflecting on capital punishment prior to his making 'A Short Film About Killing'. He said that the practice was 'being done in my name' and 'I am a member of this society' as indications of his own sense of responsibility for what he saw as a barbaric and unjustified practice. It is this sense of identification with the political community of which one is a member which is central to understanding political obligation.

It is this understanding of what it is to be a member of a polity, for example, which explains the very real difference between the relationship of British and American citizens to the United States' involvement in the war in Vietnam: a difference which was in this respect independent of attitudes of support or opposition. This might be expressed briefly, glossing over a great many historical complexities, by saying that the United States was responsible for waging that war while Britain was not. And while many Americans who actually opposed the war, perhaps paradoxically if one thinks only of personal responsibility, came to feel a deep sense of *shame* and even *guilt* about what was being done in Vietnam, British citizens could feel *anger* or even *outrage* at it, but *shame* or *guilt* only in so far as Britain was implicated through its support for American policy. Of course, nothing depends upon this choice of example and it would not be difficult to find others, if the historical interpretation of this one is regarded as unduly tendentious.

The general point is that such feelings of shame and guilt (and also pride) are readily intelligible in respect of the actions of the polity of which one is a member but they logically cannot be experienced in the same way about the actions of other polities. (The matter is a little more complicated than this suggests. It is, for example, possible to identify with the whole of humankind; as in the thought, 'it made me ashamed to be human'. This does not present any serious problems for the argument here, though it does indicate the kind of complexity which would need to be accommodated in a fuller statement of it.) Furthermore, while the extent of one's support for, or active opposition to, the actions of one's polity may modify or qualify these feelings, such opposition or support does not exhaust the sense of an intelligible relationship of responsibility for those actions. This sense of identity and the corresponding responsibility is part of what it means to be a member of a polity and to recognise one's political obligations.

Nor, it should be noticed, is this sense of identity and corresponding responsibility just something which is experienced only from the point of view of the individual member of the polity. It is not, therefore, *merely* a subjective feeling. Both the government of the political community of which one is a member and the members and governments of other polities will in many contexts employ a similar understanding. The government of one's own polity, and indeed other members of it will characteristically expect some recognition of this shared identity and the acknowledgement of some allegiance to the community. The governments of other polities will not regard the claims on their resources of non-members in the same light as those of members. Members of a polity will often be treated as sharing collective political responsibility for the actions of that polity. For example, war reparations may be sought from another polity, regardless of the fact that many of the people who will suffer as a result were opposed to the war for which the reparations are demanded. None of this is intended to deny the importance of personal responsibility, or that there are many circumstances in which it would be wrong or inappropriate to invoke a shared identity and common responsibility. It may be correct to have held the Germans or Japanese people of 1945 collectively responsible for the war, and to impose collective sanctions and penalties upon them; but it would be mistaken to hold them similarly responsible for the particular atrocities committed by individual concentration camp guards. I wish to show only that notions of a shared political identity and collective political responsibility do function routinely in the morality of political life. The recognition of such an identity and the corresponding responsibility is internally connected to our acknowledging our political obligations.

Although an attempt has been made to show that the kinds of thoughts and emotions within which our understanding of political obligation should be situated are not merely subjective notions or feelings, this will not satisfy some critics. One reply to my claims which is likely to be made by both the philosophical anarchists and proponents of traditional theories of political obligation is that, though it may as a matter of fact be true that we do think and feel about the polity of which we are members in the way I have described, no moral justification of these responses has been offered. Here differences about what can legitimately be expected of political philosophy are likely to be to the fore. If such thoughts and feelings are shown to be morally intelligible in the context of a shared identity, constituted by membership of a particular polity, why is more necessary? Why do such thoughts and feelings have to be shown to be justified in terms of consent, the principle of fairness, utilitarianism or some other preferred moral theory? What kind of 'justification' does political obligation stand in need of and what can political philosophy supply? Once we come to see the intelligibility and understand the appropriateness of the ways in which we think and feel about our membership of a polity, what further moral justification is required? Of course, it may be that the account offered here completely fails in its task, but that is to raise a different objection; the point at issue in this dispute concerns the nature of that task. While the scattered remarks in this book certainly do not settle the issue, nor are they intended to, my intention is to suggest a rather different way of thinking about what it might mean to give a philosophical account of political obligation than that which is generally dominant.

As an instance of the kind of issues at stake in this dispute it may be helpful to focus on one aspect of the account of political obligation which has been offered so far, and which critics may be especially inclined to reject. They will claim that what my account shows is (at best) that people have certain 'institutional' or 'positional' obligations by virtue of their membership of a polity, but it does not follow that these are morally binding (Stocker, 1970; Simmons, 1979; Green, 1988). Institutional affiliations, such as being a member of a polity, may 'have an identificatory function in showing which duties their incumbent has, but they have no justificatory function in grounding those duties' (Green, 1988, p. 211). Or as A. J. Simmons bluntly expresses the point:

'The existence of a positional duty (i.e., someone's filling a position tied to certain duties) is a morally *neutral* fact. If a positional duty is binding on us, it is because there are grounds for a moral requirement to perform that positional duty which are independent of the position and the scheme which defines it. The existence of a positional duty, then, never establishes (by itself) a moral requirement' (Simmons, 1979, p. 21).

This argument is usually thought to be clinched by pointing to some unjust institution or role, perhaps slavery or a concentration camp guard, and asking rhetorically whether we really believe that the slave or the concentration camp guard are morally obligated to perform their institutional or positional duties. However, as I shall try to show, this argument proceeds altogether too quickly.

The first point to observe is simply that, at least in some instances, we do appear to regard positional duties as morally binding without reference to some further moral principle or theory. To revert once again to the example of the family: it is often sufficient to point out that a man is this boy's father to attribute certain obligations on the part of the man towards the boy. It is both unnecessary and misleading to seek some further moral justification for the obligations. But what, then, to come to the crucial question of institutions or roles which impose duties that we would think of as unjust or immoral? The important point to recognise here is that accounts of 'institutional' or 'positional' duties do not need to assume that these exist in a moral vacuum. Other moral principles or rules may indeed show a particular institution to be immoral, or a particular duty attached to an otherwise unobjectionable institution to be unjust, but this is not to concede the point of the critics of the claim that institutional obligations may be morally binding without further moral justification. It is one thing to show that a particular institution does not violate other fundamental moral principles or commitments, but quite another to have to show that the institution is *justified* by these other moral principles. Nor is this a unique feature of non-voluntarily acquired institutional obligations. Thus, for example, if Fred promises Mary to murder John, Fred acquires no obligation to murder John, for it was not something Fred was entitled to promise, and Mary has no right to its enactment. (It is a mistake in this kind of case to say that Fred has a *prima facie* obligation to commit the murder, or that his obligation to Mary is overridden by the moral prohibition on murder. Fred simply has no moral obligation to murder John, whatever he may have promised Mary.) Institutions which give rise to moral obligations also exist within a wider context of other moral beliefs and commitments. These may set various limits to the moral obligations to which institutions can legitimately give rise, but this is not to justify those institutions or the corresponding obligations in terms of those other moral considerations. Political obligation cannot include within it the obligation to commit murder (see Anscombe, 1978), but this does not mean that a polity, or the corresponding political obligation, is, or needs to be, justified by the moral prohibition on murder. Of course if it were shown, as for example most anarchists try to, that political obligation regularly violated other fundamental moral commitments, then this would be a serious objection to any defence of it, but this is not the argument of those critics of positional or institutional moral obligations that have been considered here.

Finally, before leaving this issue, it should be observed that not all institutions or institutional obligations are on a par with each other. Some institutions play a role so fundamental in our lives that they are partly constitutive of our self-understanding, or our sense of who we are. A woman may, for example, belong to her local tennis club and this may impose certain institutional obligations on her, but those obligations, even where they are moral, will not normally be constitutive of her sense of identity. (I leave aside the different case of the woman who 'lives for her local tennis club'.) If she disapproves of what is happening in the club or if she grows bored with tennis then she can leave and join another club or take up squash instead, without raising any questions about her sense of who she is. Other institutional involvements, however, are much more closely bound up with this sense of who we are, a self-understanding which characteristically has a fundamentally moral dimension. For example, if the woman was also a devout Catholic, leaving the Church may be practically no more difficult than leaving the tennis club, but her Catholicism will be much more deeply connected to her sense of identity and is unlikely to be jettisoned without a serious reappraisal of her moral values and commitments. It should not be surprising, therefore, that some institutional obligations, through their deep-rooted connections with our sense of who we are and our place in the world, have a particularly fundamental role in our moral being. That these kinds of institutional involvement generate moral obligations, and that these obligations rather than standing in need of justification may themselves be justificatory, is only to be expected. In the case of political obligation, however, there are other problems to which this account might reasonably be thought to give rise.

Thus a more worrying objection to this account of political obligation might come from a more sympathetic or generously disposed critic who, while conceding that the thoughts and feelings discussed have been shown to be intelligible and plausible, may doubt that they have been shown to be in any sense necessary. It will be agreed that people *may* make sense of their membership of a polity in the manner indicated, but *must* they do so? What, for example, of someone who simply does not recognise a common identity with fellow members and correspondingly denies any political obligations? Of course, such a person may be denying different things. For example, it may be that all moral obligations or duties are being denied and we are facing that familiar figure in moral philosophy, the amoralist. In challenging all morality, though, the amoralist raises questions which, were we to pursue them, would take us too far from our present purposes. In any case the amoralist (unlike the immoralist) is to be found much more in the pages of philosophy books than in life. More interestingly, however, it may be that only specifically political obligation is being denied, and it is this interpretation of the objection which merits particular attention. The problem which this objection identifies may be thought to arise from the contention that obligations are internally related to membership of a polity and that such membership is not normally voluntarily assumed. Thus, though membership of a particular polity is not usually chosen, it does not follow that it cannot be rejected or renounced. As, for example, the facts of emigration and naturalisation attest, it is possible to cease to be a member of one polity and to become a member of another. The real problem, therefore, is not whether it is possible for a person to exchange an obligation to one polity for an obligation to another, but whether political obligation can be altogether denied: that is, can the standard conditions of membership be met, yet there be no corresponding obligations?

Membership and political obligation

The question which now needs to be addressed is that of whether people can renounce or deny their political obligations while remaining, at least from the point of view of the other members and in terms of generally accepted criteria, members of their polity. In this context the analogy with the family is unilluminating. Parents may 'disown' their children, and sons or daughters may 'deny' their parents but, where this is more than rhetoric, relations between those concerned will more or less effectively cease. The kind of dissassociation from family life which this involves is tolerably clear. However, the relations which comprise membership of a polity are much less easy to escape, at least while remaining resident within its territory. In large part, therefore, what needs to be clarified is what counts as 'membership' of a polity, and how and under what circumstances this can be repudiated. There is a limit to what can be said about this in general terms, but certainly the presence or absence of a more or less conscious identification with one's polity and the corresponding acknowledgement of one's obligations to other members of the political community will be crucial so far as the perception of the individual is concerned.

The argument about political obligation developed so far has been basically twofold. First, there is the conceptual claim that political obligation is a feature of membership of a polity without which the very idea of 'membership' is unintelligible. Secondly, it has been argued that persons' recognition of themselves as members of a polity shows itself in certain characteristic ways of thinking and feeling about their polity; that these thoughts and feelings are clearly intelligible; and that they are neither voluntarily assumed, nor stand in need of justification in terms of some fundamental moral principle or theory. However, nothing in what has been said implies that persons *must* think and feel about 'their polity' in the manner indicated; only that if they do this is a manifestation of their recognition of themselves as members of a particular polity. In recognising themselves as members they also acknowledge themselves as having corresponding political obligations. The possibility that we must now consider is that some people do not have the kinds of thoughts and feelings associated with membership of a political community. If this is so, do such people lack political obligations?

The first point to make is that lacking these thoughts and feelings is not the same as claiming to lack them. If people do lack them this will be apparent not merely in what they say but in how they act. Indeed, it is a feature of my account of political obligation that the mere denial of political obligation, as is sometimes to be encountered in philosophical discussion, should not be taken at face value. Though explicitly denied, such obligations may be implicitly acknowledged through the many and various ways in which membership of a polity is recognised and observed. To participate fully and actively in the political life of a community; conscientiously to observe the rules and standards of the community; and generally, over a sustained period of time, consistently to behave in ways indistinguishable from those recognised as appropriate for a member of the political community; but then to deny that one acknowledges any political obligations lacks conviction. Rejecting political obligation requires detaching oneself from a complex web of practices, beliefs and emotions associated with membership of a political community. It is likely that when most denials of political obligation are examined it will be discovered that they are more or less disingenuous; but it must be conceded that they may not always be so, and it is not clear that philosophical argument could show that they must be.

There is, as I shall explain shortly, one very large and important class of cases where identifying and attributing political obligations is especially difficult, and sometimes perhaps impossible. What, though, of our potential dissident, who meeting the kinds of conditions specified above, denies having any political obligations to the polity which claims him or her as a member. In such rare cases we are, I believe, simply confronted with conflicting perspectives, and, though the political philosopher can usefully characterise and explore these different perspectives, there may be no way ultimately to adjudicate between them. In extreme cases – for example that of an unworldly hermit whose understanding of himself lacks any sense of identity with the political community and who exists as far as possible apart from it – it may even be that the political community should recognise that it has no authority over such a person and no reciprocal obligations obtain. In such exceptional cases the political community will have the right to protect itself against any serious infraction of its rules and standards, but it may have no legitimate claims on his allegiance and he should, by and large, be left alone. However, it is clear that these kinds of case really are exceptional, and they do not to any significant extent impugn the account of political obligation which I have given. Nor does another unusual kind of case – that where some people identify themselves as members of a particular political community but this identification is denied by at least a large proportion of the other members of the polity with which they identify. These too are a complication, but not an embarrassment, and, therefore, they will not be pursued further here.

One further possible objection to the argument which needs to be considered relates to that large and important class of difficult cases I referred to earlier. This objection might concede that the argument has some merit when applied to polities with a fairly stable and continuous existence and in which the question of who are and are not members is largely unproblematic, but deny its relevance to those not uncommon situations in which there is widespread dispute about the identity of a polity and about who should be recognised as members of it. The examples are numerous and include Republicans in Northern Ireland, Basques in Spain, Kurds in Iraq, the Palestinian question and the post-war history of parts of the Indian subcontinent, to mention only a few of the more recent cases. Any adequate account of political obligation, it might reasonably be argued, should have something more illuminating to say about these kinds of case than the account defended here seems able to supply. Perhaps in some respects this is so, but it is worth entering some caveats.

First, these cases are less of an embarrassment than might be thought, for it is surely a virtue of any account of political obligation that it has at least *some* difficulty with them. There would most certainly be something wrong with any account which found them straightforward and unproblematic, since where the integrity of the polity is itself subject to widespread and fundamental dispute, political identity and political obligation are likely to be uncertain and confused. Second, even an account of political obligation which was limited in its validity to polities where identity was not seriously disputed would be a worthwhile achievement. Third, my account of political obligation is at least illuminating about why these sorts of cases are difficult. Once we understand, for example, the importance of a shared sense of political identity, we can see how its absence will radically undermine any coherent representation of political obligations. In this way, pursuing the logic of this account helps to locate the source of what is problematic about political obligation in these difficult cases. Finally, the disputes which such examples characteristically involve are not of a nature such that the philosopher can resolve them, and it is only if we continue to believe that this is the task of political philosophy that we shall think of our inability to do so as a failure.

Law, government and political obligation

So far the argument has attempted to show, partly through an extended comparison with the family, how political obligation can be understood as an essential concomitant of membership of a polity and that, since membership does not normally result from a voluntary undertaking, nor *a fortiori* will political obligation. Additionally, part of what is involved in membership of a polity has been elucidated through an exploration of how concepts and feelings such as guilt, shame, pride and responsibility make sense in such a context: how they enter into our attitudes and deliberations as citizens. This explanation of political obligation in terms of membership and a shared identity, therefore, also enables us to account for the particular claims on people of their own polity. It is precisely that it is *their* political community which gives them a distinctive reason for action, which they lack with respect to other polities. Of course this is not to deny that they will often have many other reasons to attend to the claims of their, and of other, polities; but it does identify what is distinctive to political obligation – which is that it is owed only to the particular polity of which they are members. However, we are now in a position to say a little more about the content of political obligation and particularly how it relates to government and law.

An especially important, and probably controversial, aspect of political obligation as it is understood here is that it is not simply a matter of obedience to the law and the government. It is categorically not an implication of the argument that political obligation always requires us to obey the law or the government. This might be thought to be a peculiarly perverse contention, for the problem of political obligation, as was indicated in Chapter 1, has often been understood to be just the problem of why one should obey the government or law. However, obedience must be distinguished from obligation, and obedience to law or government is not the only possible manifestation of political obligation; though in many circumstances it is likely to be especially compelling, and probably must be the norm. As I shall explain, not all laws or governments are authoritative, and even when they are, it does not follow that they must always be obeyed.

What political obligation, in the most general terms, does require is that people's actions take account of the interests or welfare of their polity: a conception which is constituted through their sharing an identity as members of that polity. To be a member is to be related in a particular way to other members of the polity. Any account of the content of political obligation must be directed towards an understanding of that relationship. In very general terms, therefore, political obligation is structured through that relationship and must involve some concern for the interests or welfare of the polity of which one is a member. Again, though, it is necessary to warn against a possible misunderstanding of this point. The expression 'the interests and welfare of the polity' is open to a wide variety of interpretations and should not be taken either to imply or to require any general substantive account, philosophical or otherwise, of what the interests and welfare of the polity *must* consist in. Thus it offers no support for utilitarianism or for any philosophically preferred substantive conception of the common good. This may make the argument seem disappointingly empty, and while it must be conceded that 'having regard to the interests and welfare of the polity' is vague and lacks specificity, it is possible to say a little more about it even at this level of generality. Although political obligation does not entail any particular, precisely specifiable actions, it is not vacuous. A further comparison with the family may begin to help us to see how this is so.

The obligations people have to their parents or siblings are also indeterminate, but taking account of the interests and welfare of parents and siblings is nonetheless a real and meaningful activity. There may be much room for dispute about the extent of such obligations and whether a particular action fulfills them, but such disagreement is not infinitely open and not anything, in a particular context, can be understood as fulfilling familial obligations. Much the same is true of political obligation. Am I required to fight on behalf of my polity, to pay taxes, to seek to change an unjust law or to oppose a particular foreign policy initiative? How much am I required to do? These are not questions to which any general account of political obligation can provide a once and for all answer: both the nature of the particular polity of which one is a member and the precise circumstances in which such questions are asked are crucial to how they are answered. There are inevitably many actions, choices and decisions, including many moral ones, in which our political obligation may quite properly play no explicit role: a host of everyday activities may be carried on to which our political obligations form no more than an unconscious background. Political obligations provide but one part of the conceptual structure within which deliberation about what to do takes place: sometimes they will be the explicit focus of deliberation or directly enter into it, but at others they will not. Again the parallel with familial obligations should be apparent.

Moreover, as should be clear from the discussion so far, all obligations exist in a context of other, often conflicting or competing, obligations. Nothing in the account offered here presumes either that all our obligations are ultimately harmonious or, equally importantly, that political obligations must have primacy over other moral obligations. Just as obligations to parents may be overridden by, for example, those to a wife or husband, friends, a business partner, the unjustly imprisoned and so on, so political obligations, too, may be similarly over-ridden. However, neither does this account deny that, on occasion, under particular circumstances political obligation may have primacy. Sometimes, moreover, a political obligation may conflict tragically with other moral obligations: one such instance is the case of Antigone, as presented in Sophocles' play, forbidden by Creon her acknowledged and rightful ruler from burying her rebellious dead brother, Polynices, as familial duty and piety required. Beyond such commonplaces it is doubtful whether philosophy can say anything useful of a general nature about the precise weight to be attached to political obligations, though the account offered here should help us to see why in many circumstances they are likely to be weighty. If our membership of a polity has the kind of place in our lives which this account suggests, then the obligations associated with it will need to be regarded with some seriousness.

So far, it might be objected, several claims have been made about what political obligation is not, but little has been said positively about its content. As should be apparent from the nature of the argument I have advanced, there is a significant limit to what can be said about its content in general terms. Political obligation is associated with membership of a particular political community, and it is the specific characteristics of each community which determine what political obligation will require. However, it would be unsatisfactory to leave the matter quite so open, and it is surely true that more needs to be said, in particular, about the relationship of political obligation to law and to government. It is, therefore, to this task that the remainder of this section will be devoted.

In fact most of the elements necessary to characterise this relationship are already in place. What needs to be added is that the sense of identity which is constituted through membership of a particular polity is most naturally expressed through the acknowledgement of the authority of its laws and government. It is these which characteristically define the terms of association within a polity. Concern for the interests and welfare of the polity is a concern for these terms of association. To be a member of a particular political community is standardly to recognise the authority of its laws (or sometimes more informally its customs) and its government. It may involve more – a theocratic polity may, for example, effectively require its members to subscribe to a particular religious belief, not in the sense that it is a legal requirement (though it might be), but because the laws and government of that community would make little sense unless members shared those religious convictions. More problematically, as I shall go on to explain, political obligation may involve less; but paradigmatically it requires the recognition of the right of the government to rule and acknowledgement of the claims on conduct of the law. This is the core of the content of political obligation. It does not assume that all polities must conform to one generally ethically preferred constitutional structure, such as liberal democracy, but neither does it assume that people are always required to act in accordance with the law. Acknowledging political obligations does not preclude conscientious disobedience to laws, or even in some, admittedly unusual, instances the denial that the actual government is authoritative. These latter denials might be thought specially puzzling, and I shall further elucidate the relationship of political obligation to both law and government by explaining them.

To deal with the more straightforward point first; acknowledging the authority of the law does not require that all laws must be obeyed. There are at least two different kinds of circumstances in which disobedience to the law may be consistent with acknowledging one's political obligation. First, particular laws may not have been made in accordance with the established legal procedures, or other legitimate processes,· of that political community. Such laws may be unconstitutional, *ultra vires*, contrary to accepted principles of natural justice without good cause, and so on. In this way, perhaps, they might be deemed not to be laws at all, but the important point is not terminological: it is that such 'laws' or commands are not authoritative; and though a government may seek, and have the power, to enforce them, people are under no obligation to take account of them in their deliberations. Secondly, and more interestingly, the law may be recognised as authoritative, even when disobeying a specific procedurally valid law. The most familiar instance of this is the classic conception of civil disobedience (Cohen, 1971). The civil disobedient acknowledges the authority of the law and the government's right to enforce it, by willingly accepting punishment for the infraction of the law. Moreover, these two kinds of case are exemplary, rather than claimed as exhaustive of the possibilities: there may well be other ways of acknowledging the authority of laws while disobeying some of them. Additionally, and more tentatively, it may even be possible for a person to invoke his or her political obligation as a reason for disobeying this or that law. Obviously *political* obligation cannot normally consist in pervasive and consistent disobedience to the laws of one's polity, but where, for example, a particular law is demonstrably radically at variance with the prevailing structure of law, one might appeal to the integrity of the political community as itself a reason for disobedience (see Dworkin, 1986, Ch. 6). Certainly such instances are problematic, and even more certainly they cannot be the norm; but it is far from clear that they are impossible.

What though of the still more apparently paradoxical claim that political obligation may be consistent with denying the authority of the *de facto* government of one's polity? This possibility results from a gap that can arise between acknowledging the authority of the law and recognising the authority of a government. For example, what if the effective government attained power by unlawful means? This case is like that of an invalid law, but more radical in its implications. A good historical example might be that of the Vichy government in wartime France. Most French citizens did not recognise the Vichy government as having political authority, yet they can sensibly be said to have retained their sense of belonging to the French state. They could plausibly claim that their political obligations not only implied no recognition of the authority of the Vichy government, but that it actually required opposition to it. (Of course there were other moral reasons for resistance but these are not to the point in this context.) Many French citizens recognised the authority of the De Gaulle government in exile, yet they also will have acknowledged the authority of much of the law, left unchanged by the government of usurpation. In this situation political obligation seems entirely consistent with the denial of the authority of the *de facto* government; but how long an intelligible sense of *political* obligation could survive this sundering from the effective government of the community is a moot point.

Epitaph for political obligation?

This last point, however, gestures towards a much more fundamental problem – a problem all the more disturbing because it is raised by a philosopher who might be expected to be broadly sympathetic to the account of political obligation that has been defended in this chapter. It is a problem which arises from the claim that under the conditions of modernity – conditions of pervasive ethical diversity and pluralism within polities – there is no political community because the essential precondition of moral consensus is absent. Hence there can be no political obligation since government is only a bureaucratic imposition which has no moral claims on its subjects. In the words of Alasdair MacIntyre:

'In any society where government does not express or represent the moral community of the citizens, but is instead a set of institutional arrangements for imposing a bureaucratic unity on a society which lacks genuine moral consensus, the nature of political obligation becomes systematically unclear. Patriotism is or was a virtue founded on attachment primarily to a political and moral community and only secondarily to the government of that community; but it is characteristically exercised in discharging responsibility to and in such government. When however the relationship of government to the moral community is put in question both by the changed nature of government and the lack of moral consensus in the society, it becomes difficult any longer to have any clear, simple and teachable conception of patriotism.

Loyalty to my country, to my community – which remains
unalterably a central virtue – becomes detached from obedience to
the government which happens to rule me' (MacIntyre, 1981, pp.
236–7).

Of course in many respects this passage is entirely consistent with
my account of political obligation: MacIntyre too regards political
obligation as rooted in a shared identity constitutive of a political
community. However, for him this has to be underpinned by a
substantive moral consensus which is singularly lacking in modern
societies. How serious a problem is this for my account of political
obligations as it applies to the modern state?

It is, I believe, a challenge which deserves to be treated with
respect, but it is not one to which it is impossible to respond. In
particular there are three points to be made in reply. First,
MacIntyre's claim can be partially conceded without the concession
being too damaging. Political obligation probably is more unclear in
modern states than in small, culturally and morally homogeneous
societies. We do, indeed, live in a much more morally complex and
complicated (though not necessarily morally richer) world, but this
does not render political obligation meaningless, only more difficult
to determine. Secondly, one can take issue with the conclusions
MacIntyre appears to draw from the ethically diverse (in his view
ultimately ethically incoherent) nature of modern societies. Such
moral diversity and pluralism is a significant feature of these
societies – a point made earlier in criticising T. H. Green's theory
of political obligation – but it does not follow that from the various
different moral perspectives there cannot be some agreement about
the desirability of many laws, or even where there is such disagreement that there cannot be some mutual accommodation which, if
less than ideal, is still generally acceptable. Some substantive
disagreements will persist, and some may be serious, but such is
politics. Moreover, it is interesting to observe how little, for
example, in a religiously and ethnically plural society such as
modern Britain, these differences translate into political conflicts.
The major political divisions between the Labour and Conservative
parties map very poorly on to the kind of ethical disagreements
about abortion, for example, which so exercise MacIntyre. One
reason for this is that one can be deeply and genuinely ethically

committed on an issue and yet not seek to impose one's view through legislation.

This last observation leads naturally to the final point which is that MacIntyre greatly exaggerates the need for a deep and pervasive moral consensus to underpin political obligation. The lack of such a consensus will undoubtedly affect the broad character of a particular political community, but so long as that character is reflected in its political institutions and laws then there need be no bar to the acknowledgement of the authority of its laws and government. It is this which is fundamental to political obligation, and this need not depend upon any deep and pervasive underlying moral consensus. To borrow Michael Oakeshott's evocative expression political obligation may require no more than 'a watery fidelity' on the part of those acknowledging the authority of their government and the laws of their polity. Yet is must be conceded that the fidelity cannot afford to become too watery lest it be dissolved entirely. If it were true that the modern state is no more than a kind of Hobbesian war of all against all, as MacIntyre sometimes explicitly suggests in *After Virtue*, then political obligation would indeed be deeply problematic. Although this picture of the modern state is a caricature, it is a caricature of a recognisable reality. The process of moral fragmentation which MacIntyre so eloquently charts must have a tendency to undermine a sense of political identity, weaken the bonds of membership and hence imperil political obligation. So the threat of fragmentation and dissolution to political obligation is a real one, though MacIntyre's obituary for it is surely premature.

In summary, this chapter has argued that political obligation is conceptually connected to membership of a particular polity; that membership of a polity is not usually a matter of choice or voluntary commitment; that neither membership nor the corresponding obligations normally require further moral justification; that the connection between membership and obligation is mediated through a sense of (partial) identification with the political community; that political obligation requires taking account of the interests and welfare of one's polity; that political obligation is particularly closely connected to acknowledging the authority of the law and government of one's polity which is the kernel of the terms of political association; and that recognition of this authority is consistent with particular acts of disobedience. Several objections to this account have been considered, but none has been found sufficiently compelling to require its rejection. It has been a particular concern to provide an account which dispenses with the claims of voluntarism without succumbing to philosophical anarchism. It is, however, acknowledged that the account of political obligation defended in this chapter is no more than a sketch, requiring further elaboration both in general and, more importantly, in the context of specific political communities.

The argument has further sought to exemplify a rather different approach to and interpretation of the problem of political obligation from that which is common in most of the philosophical literature. Finding the standard theories of political obligation and the scepticism of the philosophical anarchists equally unsatisfactory; building in part upon a genuine insight of proponents of the conceptual argument while seeking to avoid their errors; a somewhat different way of thinking about political obligation has been set out. No doubt the articulation of this approach has introduced difficulties of its own, and I shall return to some of the methodological questions to which it gives rise in the Conclusion; but, whatever the defects of execution, it might be useful to mention at least some of its virtues. It avoids what now appears to be the blind alley of many of the more traditional approaches to the moral justification of political obligation. It directs our attention to a rather different set of questions, such as the nature of a polity and the meaning of membership and to a more interpretative, yet not necessarily uncritical, way of thinking about our moral and political experience. It recognises both the complexity of political affairs and the limits of what it is reasonable to expect from political philosophy; and it seeks an account of political obligation which relates it not to some ideal world only distantly connected with our world, but to our recognisable experience of political life with its attendant imperfections and complexities. It represents a move away from that 'atomistic individualism' which has been the bane of so much contemporary political philosophy and offers scope for an account of political phenomena, such as political obligation, which is more hospitable to our actual experience of them. However, in all these respects what has been set out here is no more than a

beginning; hopefully, a beginning which others may find sufficiently interesting to want to take further, and in the process
correct and revise the errors which this preliminary account no
doubt contains. In the Conclusion, I shall briefly offer some
tentative reflections on alternative conceptions of moral and
political philosophy.

7   Conclusion

The main tasks of this book have now been completed. Several philosophical theories of political obligation have been discussed and evaluated, and a more promising alternative account has been sketched. The presentation of that alternative account is admittedly underdeveloped, though its broad outlines should be reasonably clear. Certainly it would benefit from a fuller statement even in general terms, but more particularly it indicates the need for a more detailed exploration of political obligation in the context of specific political communities. It is primarily this kind of enquiry which will produce a richer and more complex understanding of the various ways in which political obligation structures and enters into people's practical deliberations, and the role it plays in the life of different political communities. However, this is as far as the enquiry into political obligation will be taken in the present book.

There is, however, one underlying issue to which it would be appropriate to return in this conclusion, by way of a coda to the specific arguments about political obligation. This issue concerns the conception of political philosophy that the account of political obligation which has been defended seeks to exemplify. This chapter, therefore, will be taken up with a few brief reflections on the nature of the methodological assumptions underlying this account. I shall try to characterise my approach and contrast it with an alternative which has had, and continues to have, greater currency within moral and political philosophy, though I make no claims to originality. However, I shall not seek to *resolve* any of the fundamental questions to which such an enquiry gives rise; and in this respect it will be a perhaps inappropriately inconclusive conclusion.

In the opening chapter I wrote of a 'mismatch' between the kind of account of political obligation advanced and defended in Chapter 6 and the theories considered in earlier chapters. The nature of this mismatch should by now be rather clearer. The account of political obligation which I have articulated does not seek to provide a general justification of political obligation, whether in terms of some more or less specific moral principles or some more or less comprehensive moral theory. In this respect the account presented is not strongly normative: for example, it certainly does not aspire to develop a set of necessary and sufficient conditions for determining whether, or how far, people are morally obliged to act in accordance with what the laws and government to which they are subject require. Of course not all earlier philosophical theories claim to have achieved this, yet it is, I believe, this aspiration which is predominant in the way in which those theories are currently assessed within Anglo-American political philosophy. Indeed, by not even attempting to meet these criteria, it will seem to many contemporary philosophers that this account is woefully inadequate, and perhaps does not qualify as a *philosophical* account of political obligation at all. What kind of conception of philosophy, then, is it supposed to exhibit?

In part the answer to this question was given in Chapter 1 when discussing the nature of philosophy as conceptual enquiry. In that context, however, it was appropriate to present a characterisation of political philosophy which was inclusive; and which incorporated within it the broad variety of approaches that political philosophers have in fact employed. In this conclusion, by contrast my point is to identify the differences between most theories of political obligation (at least as they have standardly come to be understood) and the approach which I have sought to defend. The main substance of these differences is illuminatingly articulated by Bernard Williams when discussing moral philosophy more generally, and it is worth quoting him at some length. He writes:

'There could be a way of doing moral philosophy that started from the ways in which we experience our ethical life. Such a philosophy would reflect on what we believe, feel, take for granted; the ways in which we confront obligations and recognise responsibility; the sentiments of guilt and shame. It would involve a phenomenology of ethical life. This could be good philosophy, but it would be unlikely to yield an ethical theory. Ethical theories, with their concern for tests, tend to start from just one aspect of ethical experience, beliefs. The natural understanding of an ethical theory takes it as a structure of propositions, which, like a scientific theory, in part provides a framework for our beliefs, in part criticizes or revises them. So it starts from our beliefs, though it may replace them' (Williams, 1985, p. 93).

It should be apparent that the approach adopted in this book bears some significant similarities to that which Williams calls a 'phenomenology of the ethical life', whereas the accounts which have been criticised share more with what he calls 'ethical theories'. There are, however, two potential misunderstandings which might arise from this characterisation which it would be well to dispel, and which will help to fill out this account.

First, to reiterate a point which has been made earlier, a phenomenology of ethical life need not be entirely uncritical. Our ordinary ethical beliefs, feelings and assumptions may be incoherent, contradict each other, or be disordered in other respects. In this way a phenomenology of ethical life can retain significant critical purchase on that ethical life. What it does not do, however, by contrast with an ethical theory, is claim to be able to provide a replacement for a disordered ethical life, if such it turns out to be. It may help us in revising our beliefs or in trying to restructure some of our moral emotions; by showing which beliefs or feelings are most incongruous or aberrant; by drawing out implications or revealing assumptions of those beliefs or feelings which would lead an agent to doubt their cogency or viability; or by a series of other interpretative or hermeneutic techniques. Such a moral phenomenology, however, cannot claim to be possessed of some substantive moral truth which the ordinary moral agent is then expected to substitute for error. It is in this sense that Williams is right to say that a moral phenomenology is not an ethical *theory*, though there is a looser sense of theorising – as systematic, general reflection – in which such an approach can quite properly be regarded as theoretical.

The second potential misunderstanding would be to think that, because of these differences of approach, what Williams calls 'ethical theories' can have nothing to contribute to a phenomenology of ethical life. This would be a mistake, because ethical theories themselves frequently include a more or less substantial phenomenological component. As Williams says, most ethical theories at least start from some genuine, if limited, aspect of our ethical experience. Thus, for example, some common good theories, in so far as they are interpretative rather than prescriptive, may make a significant contribution to our understanding of political obligation. It is partly for this reason that connections can be made between the account of political obligation I have defended and those of other philosophers, who may not have shared a precisely similar philosophical approach. However, it must also be acknowledged, that these connections are more difficult to make with theories such as extreme forms of utilitarianism, which are radically, systematically and unrepentantly at variance with ordinary moral beliefs and practices. The kind of philosophical approach adopted here, therefore, is able to draw on, and learn from, the work of other philosophers whose understanding of their task is significantly different (Horton, 1990); but inevitably the work of some moral and political philosophers will be both more accessible and more helpful than that of others.

It is unlikely that much that has been presented in this book will succeed in persuading those moral and political philosophers committed to a more ambitious conception of the aim of their enquiries. However, the various considerations which have been advanced may carry some weight with the undecided, the wavering or those fresh to moral and political philosophy. Moreover, even if one does not believe that most of the traditional accounts of political obligation are necessarily doomed to failure, the widespread lack of conviction which most of them carry may encourage further reflection on the nature of the questions to which they have sought an answer. If there cannot be a convincing philosophical *theory* of political obligation, then it may not be, as for example the philosophical anarchists claim, that there are no political obligations: it may be that it is what is expected from a satisfactory account of political obligation which is mistaken. However, I cannot pretend to have provided anything close to a compelling case to justify such a contention, nor perhaps is such a thing possible (Rorty, 1989). But I do claim to have raised some genuine doubts, and, however inadequately, to have sketched an alternative: both an alternative account of political obligation and, more obliquely, and mostly through this exemplification, of political philosophy. No doubt the arguments about both will and should continue.

Guide to Further Reading

The best general introduction to political obligation is that provided by Simmons (1979). He offers excellent critical discussions of several theories of political obligation, and though my book takes issue with the philosophical anarchism which he endorses, I have learned a great deal from him. Indeed this book can be read in part as a conscious response to the challenge Simmons' work presents. Other good systematic and more or less general discussions can be found in Flathman (1972), Green (1988), Greenawalt (1987), Plamenatz (1968) and Zwiebach (1975). Briefer general discussions are provided by Dagger (1977), Dunn (1980) and (1991), and Raz (1986). Two useful collections of articles on various aspects of political obligation are those edited by Harris (1990) and Pennock and Chapman (1970). Socrates' discussion, which is perhaps the first sustained consideration of political obligation, can be found in Plato (1969) and is critically assessed by Woozley (1979).

The classic works of the social contract tradition are Hobbes (1968), Locke (1967) and Rousseau (1973). Seventeenth-century contract and consent theory is especially interestingly explored in Herzog (1989), while more extended historical discussions can be found in Gough (1967), Hampton (1986), Lessnoff (1986), Riley (1982) and Steinberg (1978). The classic critique of contract theory is Hume (1953). The best and most ingenious modern defence of consent theory is that by Beran (1977) and more fully (1987). Other recent defenders of some form of consent theory include Plamenatz (1968) and Tussman (1960). Abbott (1976) and De Lue (1989) focus specifically on liberal theorising, including consent theory; and Walzer (1970) offers some unusually stimulating reflections within the consent tradition, which are subject to critical assessment by Euben (1972). The philosophical literature on various aspects of consent and social contract theory is very extensive, and most books on political obligation include substantial discussions of it. Pateman (1985) presents perhaps the most detailed and sustained critique of consent theory; and in her (1988) and (1989) books she has explored ideas of contract and consent specifically in the context of feminist theory. Hirschmann (1989) too relates political obligation to wider feminist themes.

Political obligation is not very extensively discussed by utilitarians, other than to criticise contract and consent theory. Hume (1978) set out a proto-utilitarian account but Bentham (1988) has little to say about political obligation. In addition to the brief account in Hare (1976), criticised by Dagger (1982), Flathman (1972) provides a sustained predominantly utilitarian defence of political obligation rare among contemporary political philosophers. There exists a large number of general discussions of utilitarianism, and Lyons (1965) is especially useful on the distinction between act- and rule-utilitarianism. Green (1986) offers the classic statement of a common good theory of political obligation. It is criticised by Plamenatz (1968) and Pritchard (1968), but partially defended in Harris (1986), Milne (1962) and (1986) and Nicholson (1990). O'Sullivan (1987) discusses Green in the context of the idealist approach to political obligation more generally. Several of the essays in Harris (1990) discuss the possibilities and problems of a common good theory in a modern context.

Modern hypothetical contract theory has its origins in Kant (1991) and is defended by Pitkin (1972). 'The moral force of hypothetical consent generally is discussed in Zimmerman (1983) and Lewis (1989). The principle of fair-play is articulated by Hart (1967), further elaborated by Rawls (1964), extensively criticised in Simmons (1979), but defended by Klosko (1987). The best modern attempt to justify political obligation in terms of a principle of gratitude is that by Walker (1988) and (1989). The natural duty to support and promote just institutions is set out in Rawls (1971), and discussed in Greenawalt (1987) and Simmons (1979). A modern natural law account of political obligation is presented by Finnis (1980).

An especially helpful historical and analytical introduction to anarchism is provided by Miller (1984); while Carter (1971), Ritter (1980) and Woodcock (1963) provide further supplementation and development. Woodcock (1977) offers some useful introductory readings. Among the important works of individualist anarchism are Spooner (1966) and Tucker (1893): the modern proponents include Friedman (1973) and Rothbard (1978). Some classic statements of communal anarchism can be found in Bakunin (1972) and Kropotkin (1970). An early precursor of philosophical anarchism is Godwin (1976), but the canonical modern statement is that of Wolff (1976). Among Wolff's many critics are Bates (1972), Frankfurt (1973), Pritchard (1973), and Smith (1973b). He replies to two of them in Wolff (1973). The weaker form of philosophical anarchism is defended by Simmons (1979) and Green (1988) among others. Simmons is criticised by Klosko (1987) and Senor (1987) to whom he replies in Simmons (1987).

Students particularly interested in civil disobedience will be spoiled for choice, but might usefully consult Childress (1971), Cohen (1971), Singer (1973) or Bedau (1991). The problem of the obligation to obey the law is discussed in Carnes (1960), Mackie (1981), Raz (1979), Smith (1973), Smith (1976), and is a central topic of legal philosophy. Political authority is discussed in Anscombe (1978), De George (1985), Flathman (1980), Friedman (1973), Tuck (1972), Watt (1982) and Winch (1972a). Co-ordination problems as a foundation for political obligation are discussed in Taylor (1976). Versions of the conceptual argument are defended by MacDonald (1951), Rees (1954), McPherson (1967) and Pitkin (1972), while Pateman (1973) offers the most extensive critique of it.

Dworkin (1986) contains an interesting discussion of 'associative obligations' bearing some similarities to the account of political obligation defended in Chapter 6, though there are many important differences. Charvet (1990) also provides an account of political obligation with significant affinities to that presented here. Oakeshott (1975) offers a characteristically individual but deeply pondered account of what he calls 'civil obligation'. The moral significance of the nation state is discussed by Miller (1988) and (1989), and the relationship between the self and society is explored in Taylor (1989). Stimulating and searching critiques of much modern moral and political philosophy can be found in MacIntyre (1981), Rorty (1989), Williams (1985) and Winch (1972b). Finally, Tyler (1990) offers some empirical reflections about political obligation.

Bibliography

Abbott, P. (1976) *The Shotgun Behind the Door: Liberalism and the Problem of Political Obligation* (Athens: University of Georgia Press).

Anscombe, G. E. M. (1978) 'On the Source of the Authority of the State', *Ratio*, vol. 20.

Bakunin, M. (1972) *Bakunin on Anarchy* (1842–76) ed. S. Dolgoff (New York: Vintage Books).

Bates, S. (1972) 'Authority and Autonomy', *The Journal of Philosophy*, vol. 69.

Bedau, H. (ed.) (1991) *Civil Disobedience in Focus* (London: Routledge).

Bentham, J. (1988) *A Fragment on Government* (1776) ed. R. Harrison (Cambridge: Cambridge University Press).

Beran, H. (1976) 'Political Obligation and Democracy', *Australasian Journal of Philosophy*, vol. 50.

Beran, H. (1977) 'In Defense of the Consent Theory of Political Obligation and Authority', *Ethics*, vol. 87.

Beran, H. (1987) *The Consent Theory of Political Obligation* (London: Croom Helm).

Berry, C. J. (1986) *Human Nature* (London: Macmillan).

Brandt, R. B. (1965) 'The Concepts of Obligation and Duty', *Mind*, vol. 73.

Cameron, J. R. (1971) 'Ought and Institutional Obligation', *Philosophy*, vol. 46.

Cameron, J. R. (1971) 'The Nature of Institutional Obligation', *Philosophical Quarterly*, vol. 22.

Carnes, J. (1960) 'Why Should I Obey the Law?' *Ethics*, vol. 71.

Carritt, E. F. (1935) *Morals and Politics* (Oxford: Oxford University Press).

Carter, A. (1971) *The Political Theory of Anarchism* (London: Routledge and Kegan Paul).

Charvet, J. (1990) 'Political Obligation: Individualism and Communitarianism', in P. Harris (ed.) *On Political Obligation* (London: Routledge).

Childress, J. (1971) *Civil Disobedience and Political Obligation* (New Haven: Yale University Press).

Cohen, C. (1971) *Civil Disobedience: Conscience, Tactics and the Law* (New York: Columbia University Press).

Dagger, R. K. (1977) 'What is Political Obligation?', *American Political Science Review*, vol. 71.

Dagger, R. K. (1982) 'Harm, Utility and the Obligation to Obey the Law', *Archiv fur Recht und Social Philosophie*, vol. 68.

Daniels, N. (ed.) (1975) *Reading Rawls* (Oxford: Basil Blackwell).

De George, R. T. (1985) *The Nature and Limits of Authority* (Kansas: University of Kansas Press).

179

DeLue, S. (1989) *Political Obligation in a Liberal State* (New York: State University of New York Press).

Dunn, J. (1967) 'Consent in the Political Theory of John Locke', *Historical Journal*, vol. 10.

Dunn, J. (1980) 'Political Obligation and Political Possibilities', in his *Political Obligation in its Historical Context: Essays in Political Theory* (Cambridge: Cambridge University Press).

Dunn, J. (1991) 'Political Obligation', in D. Held (ed.) *Political Theory Today* (Oxford: Polity Press).

Dworkin, R. (1975) 'The Original Position', in N. Daniels (ed.) *Reading Rawls* (Oxford: Basil Blackwell).

Dworkin, R. (1986) *Law's Empire* (London: Fontana).

Euben, J. P. (1972) 'Walzer's *Obligations*', *Philosophy and Public Affairs*, vol. 1.

Filmer, R. (1991) *Patriarcha and Other Writings* (1680, 1685) ed. J. Sommerville (Cambridge: Cambridge University Press).

Finnis, J. (1980) *Natural Law and Natural Rights* (Oxford: Clarendon Press).

Flathman, R. (1972) *Political Obligation* (New York: Atheneum).

Flathman, R. (1980) *The Practice of Political Authority: Authority and the Authoritative* (Chicago: University of Chicago Press).

Frankfurt, H. (1973) 'The Anarchism of Robert Paul Wolff', *Political Theory*, vol. 1.

Friedman, D. (1973) *The Machinery of Freedom* (New York: Harper).

Friedman, R. B. (1973) 'On the Concept of Authority in Political Philosophy', in R. Flathman (ed.) *Concepts in Social and Political Philosophy* (New York: Macmillan).

Gaus, G. (1990) 'The Commitment to the Common Good', in P. Harris (ed.) *On Political Obligation* (London: Routledge).

Godwin, W. (1976) *Enquiry Concerning Political Justice* (1793) ed. I. Kramnick (Harmondsworth: Penguin).

Gough, J. W. (1967) *The Social Contract*, 2nd edn (Oxford: Oxford University Press).

Green, L. (1988) *The Authority of the State* (Oxford: Clarendon Press).

Green, T. H. (1986) *Lectures on the Principles of Political Obligation and Other Writings* (1881–8) eds P. Harris and J. Morrow (Cambridge: Cambridge University Press).

Greenawalt, K. (1987) *Conflicts of Law and Morality* (Oxford: Clarendon Press).

Griffin, J. (1986) *Well-Being: Its Meaning, Measurement and Moral Importance* (Oxford: Clarendon Press).

Hampton, J. (1986) *Hobbes and the Social Contract Tradition* (Cambridge: Cambridge University Press).

Hare, R. M. (1963) *Freedom and Reason* (London: Oxford University Press).

Hare, R. M. (1976) 'Political Obligation', in T. Honderich (ed.) *Social Ends and Political Means* (London: Routledge & Kegan Paul).

Hare, R. M. (1981) *Moral Thinking* (Oxford: Clarendon Press).

Harris, P. (1986) 'Green's Theory of Political Obligation and Disobedience', in A. Vincent (ed.) *The Philosophy of T. H. Green* (Aldershot: Gower).

Harris, P. (ed.) (1989) *Civil Disobedience* (Lanham: University Press of America).

Harris, P. (ed.) (1990) *On Political Obligation* (London: Routledge).

Hart, H. L. A. (1967) 'Are There any Natural Rights?' (1955), in A. Quinton (ed.) *Political Philosophy* (Oxford: Oxford University Press).

Hegel, G. W. F. (1952) *The Philosophy of Right* (1821) trans. with notes by T. M. Knox (Oxford: Clarendon Press).

Herzog, D. (1989) *Happy Slaves: A Critique of Consent Theory* (Chicago: University of Chicago Press).

Hirschmann, N. J. (1989) 'Freedom, Recognition and Obligation: A Feminist Approach to Political Theory', *American Political Science Review*, vol. 83.

Hobbes, T. (1968) *Leviathan* (1651) ed. C. B. Macpherson (Harmondsworth: Penguin).

Honoré, A. M. (1981) 'Must We Obey? Necessity as a Ground of Obligation', *Virginia Law Review*, vol. 67.

Horton, J. (1984) 'Political Philosophy and Politics', in A. Leftwich (ed.) *What is Politics? The Activity and its Study* (Oxford: Basil Blackwell).

Horton, J. (1990) 'Weight or Lightness? Political Philosophy and its Prospects', in A. Leftwich (ed.) *New Developments in Political Science* (Aldershot: Edward Elgar).

Hume, D. (1953) 'Of the Original Contract' (1742), in C. W. Hendel (ed.) *David Hume's Political Essays* (Indianapolis: Bobbs-Merrill).

Hume, D. (1978) A. *Treatise of Human Nature* (1739–40) ed. L. A. Selby-Bigge, 2nd edn rev. by P. H. Nidditch (Oxford: Clarendon Press).

Hunter, J. F. M. (1966) 'The Logic of Social Contracts', *Dialogue*, vol. 5.

Jenkins, J. (1970) 'Political Consent', *Philosophical Quarterly*, vol. 20.

Johnson, K. (1976) 'Political Obligation and the Voluntary Association Model of the State', *Ethics*, vol. 86.

Joll, J. (1971) 'Anarchism – a Living Tradition', in D. Apter and J. Joll (eds) *Anarchism Today* (London: Macmillan).

Kant, I. (1991) *Political Writings* (1784–98) ed. H. Reiss, trans. H. B. Nisbet (Cambridge: Cambridge University Press).

Kelly, P. J. (1990) *Utilitarianism and Distributive Justice: Jeremy Bentham and the Civil Law* (Oxford: Clarendon Press).

Klosko, G. (1987) 'Presumptive Benefit, Fairness and Political Obligation', *Philosophy and Public Affairs*, vol. 16.

Klosko, G. (1990) 'Parfit's Moral Arithmetic and the Obligation to Obey the Law', *Canadian Journal of Philosophy*, vol. 20.

Kropotkin, P. (1970) *Kropotkin's Revolutionary Pamphlets* (1877–1920) ed. R. N. Baldwin (New York: Dover).

Le Baron, B. (1973) 'Three Components of Political Obligation', *Canadian Journal of Political Science*, vol. 16.

Lessnoff, M. (1986) *Social Contract* (London: Macmillan).

Lewis, T. J. (1989) 'On Using the Concept of Hypothetical Consent', *Canadian Journal of Political Science*, vol. 22.

Locke, J. (1967) *Two Treatises of Government* (1690) 2nd edn, ed. by P. Laslett (Cambridge: Cambridge University Press).

Lyons, D. (1965) *Forms and Limits of Utilitarianism* (Oxford: Oxford University Press).

Lyons, D. (1981) 'Need, Necessity and Political Obligation', *Virginia Law Review*, vol. 67.

MacCormick, N. (1982) *Legal Right and Social Democracy* (Oxford: Clarendon Press).

MacDonald, M. (1951) 'The Language of Political Theory', in A. G. N. Flew (ed.) *Logic and Language*, 1st series (Oxford: Basil Blackwell).

MacIntyre, A. (1981) *After Virtue* (London: Duckworth).

Mackie, J. L. (1981) 'Obligations to Obey the Law', *Virginia Law Review*, vol. 67.

McMahon, C. (1987) 'Autonomy and Authority', *Philosophy and Public Affairs*, vol. 16.

MacPherson, C. B. (1962) *The Political Theory of Possessive Individualism* (London: Oxford University Press).

McPherson, T. (1967) *Political Obligation* (London: Routledge & Kegal Paul).

Miller, D. (1981) *Philosophy and Ideology in Hume's Political Thought* (Oxford: Clarendon Press).

Miller, D. (1983) 'Linguistic Philosophy and Political Theory', in D. Miller and L. Siedentop (eds) *The Nature of Political Theory* (Oxford: Clarendon Press).

Miller, D. (1984) *Anarchism* (London: Dent).

Miller, D. (ed.) (1987) *The Blackwell Encyclopaedia of Political Thought* (Oxford: Basil Blackwell).

Miller, D. (1988) 'The Ethical Significance of Nationality', *Ethics*, vol. 98.

Miller, D. (1989) *Market, State and Community: Theoretical Foundations of Market Socialism* (Oxford: Oxford University Press).

Milne, A. J. (1962) *The Social Philosophy of English Idealism* (London: Allen & Unwin).

Milne, A. J. (1986) 'The Common Good and Rights in T. H. Green's Ethical and Political Theory', in A. Vincent (ed.) *The Philosophy of T. H. Green* (Aldershot: Gower).

Milne, A. J. (1990) 'Political Obligation and the Public Interest', in P. Harris (ed.) *On Political Obligation* (London: Routledge).

Nicholson, P. P. (1990) *The Political Philosophy of the British Idealists* (Cambridge: Cambridge University Press).

Nickel, J. W. (1989) 'Does Basing Rights on Autonomy Imply Obligations of Political Allegiance?', *Dialogue*, vol. 28.

Norman, R. (1983) *The Moral Philosophers* (Oxford: Clarendon Press).

Nozick, R. (1974) *Anarchy, State and Utopia* (Oxford: Basil Blackwell).

Oakeshott, M. (1975) *On Human Conduct* (Oxford: Clarendon Press).

O'Sullivan, N. (1987) *The Problem of Political Obligation* (New York: Garland).

Parfit, D. (1984) *Reasons and Persons* (Oxford: Oxford University Press).

Partridge, P. (1971) *Consent and Consensus* (London: Macmillan).

Pateman, C. (1973) 'Political Obligation and Conceptual Analysis', *Political Studies*, vol. 21.

Pateman, C. (1985) *The Problem of Political Obligation: A Critique of Liberal Theory*, 2nd edn. (Oxford: Polity Press).

Pateman, C. (1988) *The Sexual Contract* (Oxford: Polity Press).

Pateman, C. (1989) *The Disorder of Women* (Oxford: Polity Press).

Pennock, J. R. and Chapman, J. W. (eds) (1970) *Nomos XII: Political and Legal Obligation* (New York: Atherton Press).

Perkins, L. (1972) 'On Reconciling Autonomy and Authority', *Ethics*, vol. 82.

Pitkin, H. (1972) 'Obligation and Consent', in P. Laslett, W. G. Runciman and Q. Skinner (eds) *Philosophy, Politics and Society*, 4th series (Oxford: Basil Blackwell).

Plamenatz, J. P. (1968) *Consent, Freedom and Political Obligation* 2nd edn (Oxford: Oxford University Press).

Plato (1969) *Crito* (395–389 BC?) trans. and intro. H. Tredennick, *The Last Days of Socrates* (Harmondsworth: Penguin).

Pritchard, H. A. (1968) *Moral Obligation and Duty and Interest* (London: Oxford University Press).

Pritchard, M. (1973) 'Wolff's Anarchism', *Journal of Value Inquiry*, vol. 7.

Proudhon, P.-J. (1979) *The Principle of Federation* (1863) trans. and intro. R. Vernon (Toronto: University of Toronto Press).

Raphael, D. D. (1976) *Problems of Political Philosophy*, rev. ed. (London: Macmillan).

Rawls, J. (1964) 'Legal Obligation and the Duty of Fair Play', in S. Hook (ed.) *Law and Philosophy* (New York: New York University Press).

Rawls, J. (1971) *A Theory of Justice* (Oxford: Oxford University Press).

Rawls, J. (1985) 'Justice as Fairness: Political not Metaphysical', *Philosophy and Public Affairs*, vol. 14.

Raz, J. (1979) *The Authority of Law* (Oxford: Clarendon Press).

Raz, J. (1986) *The Morality of Freedom* (Oxford: Clarendon Press).

Rees, J. C. (1954) 'The Limitations of Political Theory', *Political Studies*, vol. 2.

Reiman, J. (1972) *In Defense of Political Philosophy* (New York: Harper and Row).

Rhees, R. (1969) *Without Answers* (London: Routledge & Kegan Paul).

Riley, P. (1973) 'How Coherent is the Social Contract Tradition?', *Journal of the History of Ideas*, vol. 34.

Riley, P. (1982) *Will and Political Legitimacy* (Cambridge: Harvard University Press).

Ritter, A. (1980) *Anarchism: A Theoretical Analysis* (Cambridge: Cambridge University Press).

Rogowski, R. (1981) 'The Obligations of Liberalism: Pateman on Participation and Promising', *Ethics*, vol. 91.

Rorty, R. (1989) *Contingency, Irony and Solidarity* (Cambridge: Cambridge University Press).

Ross, W. D. (1930) *The Right and the Good* (London: Oxford University Press).

Rothbard, M. (1978) *For a New Liberty: The Libertarian Manifesto* (New York: Collier MacMillan).

Rousseau, J.-J. (1973) *The Social Contract* (1762) trans. and intro. M. Cranston (Harmondsworth: Penguin).

Ruben, D.-H. (1972) 'Tacit Promising', *Ethics*, vol. 83.

Sandel, M.J. (1982) *Liberalism and the Limits of Justice* (Cambridge: Cambridge University Press).

Sartorius, R. (1981) 'Political Authority and Political Obligation', *Virginia Law Review*, vol. 67.

Schochet, G.J. (1975) *Patriarchalism and Political Thought* (Oxford: Basil Blackwell).

Senor, T.D. (1987) 'What If There Are No Political Obligations? A Reply to A.J. Simmons', *Philosophy and Public Affairs*, vol. 16.

Sibley, M. (1970) 'Conscience, Law and the Obligation to Obey', *The Monist*, vol. 54.

Sidgwick, H. (1874) *The Methods of Ethics* (London: Macmillan).

Siegler, F. (1968) 'Plamenatz on Consent and Obligation', *Philosophical Quarterly*, vol. 18.

Simmons, A.J. (1979) *Moral Principles and Political Obligations* (Princeton: Princeton University Press).

Simmons, A.J. (1987) 'The Anarchist Position: A Reply to Klosko and Senor', *Philosophy and Public Affairs*, vol. 16.

Singer, P. (1973) *Democracy and Disobedience* (Oxford: Clarendon Press).

Smith, J.C. (1976) *Legal Obligation* (London: Athlone Press).

Smith, M.B.E. (1973a) 'Is There a Prima Facie Obligation to Obey the Law?', *Yale Law Journal*, vol. 82.

Smith, M.B.E. (1973b) 'Wolff's Argument for Anarchism', *Journal of Value Inquiry*, vol. 7.

Spooner, L. (1966) *No Treason: The Constitution of No Authority* (1870) (Larkspur, Col: Pine Tree Press).

Steinberg, J. (1978) *Locke, Rousseau and the Idea of Consent* (Westport: Greenwood Press).

Stirner, M. (1921) *The Ego and His Own* (1844), trans. by S. Byington (London: Jonathan Cape).

Stocker, M. (1970) 'Moral Duties, Institutions and Natural Facts', *The Monist*, vol. 54.

Taylor, C. (1975) *Hegel* (Cambridge: Cambridge University Press).

Taylor, C. (1985) *Philosophy and the Human Sciences: Philosophical Papers*, vol. 2 (Cambridge: Cambridge University Press).

Taylor, C. (1989) *Sources of the Self* (Cambridge: Cambridge University Press).

Taylor, M. (1976) *Anarchy and Co-operation* (London: Wiley).

Tuck, R. (1972) 'Why is Authority Such a Problem', in P. Laslett, W.G. Runciman and Q. Skinner (eds) *Philosophy, Politics and Society*, 4th series (Oxford: Basil Blackwell).

Tucker, B. (1893) *Instead of a Book* (New York: B.R. Tucker).

Tussman, J. (1960) *Obligation and the Body Politic* (New York: Oxford University Press).

Tyler, T. (1990) *Why People Obey the Law* (New York: Yale University Press).

Walker, A. D. (1988) 'Political Obligation and the Argument from Gratitude', *Philosophy and Public Affairs*, vol. 17.

Walker, A. D. (1989) 'Political Obligation and Gratitude', *Philosophy and Public Affairs*, vol. 18.

Walter, E. (1981) 'Personal Consent and Moral Obligation', *Journal of Value Inquiry*, vol. 15.

Walzer, M. (1970) *Obligations: Essays on Disobedience, War and Citizenship* (Cambridge, Mass: Harvard University Press).

Ward, C. (1973) *Anarchy in Action* (London: Allen & Unwin).

Wasserstrom, R. (1968) 'The Obligations to Obey the Law', in R. S. Summers (ed.) *Essays in Legal Philosophy* (Oxford: Basil Blackwell).

Watt, E. D. (1982) *Authority* (London: Croom Helm).

Weldon, T. D. (1953) *The Vocabulary of Politics* (Harmondsworth: Penguin).

Williams, B. (1973) *Problems of the Self* (London: Cambridge University Press).

Williams, B. (1985) *Ethics and the Limits of Philosophy* (London: Fontana).

Winch, P. (1972a) 'Authority and Rationality', *The Human World*, vol. 7.

Winch, P. (1972b) *Ethics and Action* (London: Routledge & Kegan Paul).

Wolff, R. P. (1973) 'Reply to Professors Pritchard and Smith', *Journal of Value Inquiry*, vol. 7.

Wolff, R. P. (1976) *In Defense of Anarchism*, 2nd edn (New York: Harper & Row).

Woodcock, G. (1963) *Anarchism* (Harmondsworth: Penguin).

Woodcock, G. (ed.) (1977) *The Anarchist Reader* (London: Fontana).

Woozley, A. D. (1979) *Law and Obedience: The Argument of Plato's Crito* (London: Duckworth).

Zimmerman, D. (1983) 'The Force of Hypothetical Commitment', *Ethics*, vol. 93.

Zwiebach, B. (1975) *Civility and Disobedience* (Cambridge: Cambridge University Press).

Index